D1417903

MONKEY
BUSINESS

MONKEY BUSINESS

7 Laws of the Jungle for Becoming
the Best of the Bunch

Sandy Wight

Mick Hager

Steve Tyink

Illustrations by Chris Sabatino

Gibbs Smith, Publisher

TO ENRICH AND INSPIRE HUMANKIND

Salt Lake City | Charleston | Santa Fe | Santa Barbara

First Edition
11 10 09 08 07   5 4 3 2 1

Text © 2007 Monkey Biz, LLC
Illustrations © 2007

All rights reserved. No part of this book may be reproduced by
any means whatsoever without written permission from the
publisher except brief portions quoted for purpose of review.

Published by
Gibbs Smith, Publisher
P.O. Box 667
Layton, Utah 84041

Orders: 1.800.835.4993
www.gibbs-smith.com

Designed by Martin Yeeles
Printed and bound in Canada

Library of Congress Cataloging-in-Publication Data

Wight, Sandra S.
   Monkey business : 7 laws of the jungle for becoming the
best of the bunch / by Sandy Wight, Mick Hager, and Steve
Tyink ; illustrations by Chris Sabatino.—1st ed.
      p. cm.
   ISBN-13: 978-1-4236-0145-6
   ISBN-10: 1-4236-0145-9
   1. Organizational behavior. 2. Customer services. 3. Suc-
cess in business. I. Hager, Mick. II. Tyink, Steve. III. Title.

HD58.7.W54 2007
658.4'09--dc22
                                    2006022200

For my sons, Chadwick and Matthew:
Kings in my heart, leaders in their world.

Sandy Wight

For Stephanie and Alex, who inspire me
by who they are becoming.

Steve Tyink

But by the grace of God . . .

Mick Hager

A Whole Bunch of Reasons . . .

Why top bananas like you need to read this book:

⭐ You want your company to be the best in the business.

⭐ You want to leave a lasting legacy of legendary leadership, rewarding results, and sustained success.

⭐ You want to create an enduring, relationship-driven, service-focused, customer-centered, fun-loving, profitable organization.

⭐ You want to be a contributing corporate citizen and give back to your community in ways that make a meaningful difference.

Why managers responsible for superior service should read this book:

⭐ You know that it isn't enough to simply satisfy your customers.

⭐ You know that you need to go the extra mile to delight your customers.

⭐ You know that consistently delighted customers become loyal, long-term fans.

⭐ You know that loyal, long-term fans will recommend your company to others, thus serving as the world's most effective advertising campaign.

What front-line service providers will gain from reading this book:

⭐ You will be known for service excellence, which will enhance your job security.

⭐ You will be an important part of something meaningful: an enduring, relationship-driven, service-focused, customer-centered, fun-loving, profitable organization.

⭐ You will create for yourself the chance to advance and prosper by consistently delighting your customers and coworkers who are serving their customers.

⭐ You will earn a solid reputation as a dedicated, seasoned, service professional, while enhancing your marketability within and outside your organization.

Service Superstars are valued, recognized, and rewarded in truly relationship-driven, customer-centered organizations.

Praise for Monkey Business

"I can't wait to see this one on the bookshelves at my favorite bookstore. This is truly amazing. As I read it, I tried to picture which animal I was and ultimately decided I had a little bit of all of them in me. This appealed to me as an adult, and it awakened my inner child as well. It was 'Monkey Magic' for my mind."

Dana Cable,
Cable & Associates, San Antonio, Texas

"A compelling blend of wisdom and creativity, *Monkey Business* is an expertly woven tale that teaches leaders how to build a business based on superior customer service. Filled with innovative tactics and practical guidance, this book is sure to help your company leap far above the jungle floor to become the best of the bunch."

Sheila L. Margolis, Ph.D., and Ava S. Wilensky, Ph.D.,
authors of There Is No Place Like Work

"Know your customers. . . . Know your star performers. That's the secret. And yet, it's just plain common sense. It's also how to do business, and that's what *Monkey Business* is all about. If you're looking for solid business principles, common sense, and more than a few good laughs along the way, read this little book. You'll be glad you did!"

John Bykowski, President & CEO
SECURA Insurance Companies
Appleton, Wisconsin

"With so much focus today on process, *Monkey Business* is a breath of fresh air in helping employees to remember their customers!"

Eric Shawger, Service Delivery Manager
GE Healthcare
Vice President—Chicago Chapter, International Customer Service Association

"*Monkey Business* is a light-hearted approach to the serious business of engaging customers and employees in a mutually beneficial relationship. Enlightening, poignant, funny, insightful, and motivational are just a few of the words that fit this message. Where can I find a full serving of *Monkey Magic*?"

Margie Weiss, Ph.D., APNP
CEO/Community Health Advocate
Neuroscience Group of Northeast Wisconsin

"Read this terrific little book and you'll understand why service is the last true differentiator in the business world. In this interesting and humorous tale, we learn the importance of connecting with customers in meaningful ways and creating personal, emotional experiences just for them. As Leader believed back then, and as winning companies do today, 'It isn't about the one big thing you do for your guests. It's about the 1000 little things that create delightful customer experiences.' In other words, sweat the small stuff."

Dr. Edward B. Harris, Service Management Program Director
University of Wisconsin–Stout
Malcolm Baldridge Award Winner
Menomonie, Wisconsin

"You have scripted the blueprint for achieving the best "Customer Experience." Congratulations for formulating a strategy in such a creative and energizing fashion. I'll be sure to share this book throughout my organization at all levels!"

Mike Weller, President
Miller Electric Manufacturing Company
Appleton, Wisconsin

"*Monkey Business* was everything I expected, and more. It was delightful, insightful, refreshing, clever, and it makes perfect business sense. I loved the characters and their witty names. The play on words in some places was so funny I laughed out loud. It is fantastic and I thoroughly enjoyed it."

Jean Ayotte, Executive Assistant to the President & CEO
SECURA Insurance Companies
Appleton, Wisconsin

"This book has the potential of being a 'home run' because it is simple, timely and powerful. It could readily lead to speaking engagements, training opportunities, and franchising. Wonderful job!"

Tom Wiltzius, Senior Vice President—Organizational Consulting
Right Management Consultants

"*Monkey Business* should be read twice. In the first read, we're amused by the humorous analogies to the animal kingdom. In the second, we're taught some truisms of successful businesses today: 'The jungle of mediocrity eats superstars for breakfast.' 'We judge ourselves on our intentions, others judge us on our words and our actions.' 'If you love what you do, you're living, not working.' 'Unless you can tell the color of your customers eyes during a face-to-face service moment, you're not fully engaged.'

"These authors are fully engaged! They know the color of our eyes. They deliver body blows of logic, lessons in employee motivation and respect, and customer satisfaction. Wight, Hager and Tyink have served up a nursery rhyme about their animal 'kingdom,' which teaches serious lessons in developing and holding customers. Through the magic of analogy and whimsy, they've written a primer on customer service the child in all of us can love."

Curtis M. Walker, Executive Director
Midwest Golf Course Owners Association
Bloomington, Minnesota

"Business people have grown to understand that we need to be re-minded more than we need to be instructed. *Monkey Business* is a good reminder for us as company leaders and those we lead."

Dave Skogen, President
Festival Foods

"I found *Monkey Business* to be a refreshing approach to supporting an organization's pursuit of reaching their strategic objectives, most importantly increased revenue through customer loyalty. The story and supporting materials are written in a way that I find most effective in getting participants to engage—fun and simple."

Kurt Johnson, Vice President—Client Services Consultant
Right Management Consultants

"This book is really good! I really like the mentions about women and how we have intuition and insight different from men. Your use of humor is right on the mark. I can see this really taking off."

Tonya Dedering, Director—Public Relations
Fox Valley Technical College
Executive Director—FVTC Foundation
Appleton, Wisconsin

"If you're looking for a great story, fascinating characters, and more than a few good laughs, you'll find them in *Monkey Business*. This amazing little book is the perfect way to learn serious business lessons during a light-hearted journey through the jungle. I took that journey and loved every minute of it!"

Sharon Hulce, President & CEO
Employment Resource Group Inc.
Appleton, Wisconsin

"*Monkey Business* is a very easy read and as the story described each type of jungle animal, I could relate that personality type to my work experiences. I also enjoyed a lot of the play on words and the puns presented throughout the book. I like the seven *Laws of the Jungle*, the need for simple profound change—getting the focus off 'me' (the employee) and on the ability of an organization to exist for the purpose of serving and maintaining relationships."

Jo Boss, Assistant Principal
Westwood Elementary School
De Pere, Wisconsin

"Monkey Business has a lot of great ideas. If I had to choose between *Who Moved My Cheese?* and *Monkey Business,* I would choose *Monkey Business.* It touches on so much more."

Carolyn Brown, High School Teacher
Notre Dame Academy
Green Bay, Wisconsin

"Not since *Who Moved My Cheese?* has the business world been treated to such a compelling story in such a clever, creative way. Like Leader in *Monkey Business,* we're all searching for the golden banana . . . the competitive edge . . . the loyal, lasting employee and customer relationships that differentiate our brand from all the rest. And, like Leader, we're learning what it takes in our quest to be the best."

"Monkey Business is an amusing, little book packed with serious business principles. Read it an hour and remember it for a lifetime!"

Catherine J. Tierney, President & CEO
Community First Credit Union
Appleton, Wisconsin

"Before I started reading this book, I thought to myself, *Does the world really need another book about customer focus?* Well, fortunately for me, I charged ahead and found I couldn't put the bloody book down! An easy, fun read that is more than just about customer focus and is right on. I know because I've seen the concepts work in real life!"

William Raaths, Chief Executive Officer
Great Northern Corporation

Contents

Foreword 16

Acknowledgments 19

Chapter 1: Monkey See, Monkey Do 20

Chapter 2: Meet Leader, Follow Leader 22

Chapter 3: These Monkeys Just Don't Get It 30

Chapter 4: Life in a Nutshell 40

Chapter 5: Laws of the Jungle 50

Chapter 6: A Monkey Business Is Born 66

Chapter 7: Now There's a Monkey Who Gets It! 78

Chapter 8: The Monkeys 3 Go to Bat and Start Swinging 82

Chapter 9: The First Monkey Wrench 88

Chapter 10: The Missing Link 100

Summary: The Tail End 106

Foreword

It's a jungle out there. That's the good news.

Can there be a better place than the jungle to learn what it takes to survive in our fiercely competitive business world? Is there a company out there that actually gets it? . . . understands that it's all about consistently creating meaningful, memorable experiences for employees and guests, thus connecting with them personally and emotionally? . . . believes in the power of building and sustaining the integrity of a brand that is really, truly different from all the others in the jungle?

Well, yes. It's right here, and it's called *Monkey Business*. Run by a team of . . . you guessed it . . . monkeys, this thriving jungle business grows from a dream in the mind of its founder, Leader, to a banana-picking empire legends are made of.

In this light-hearted, laugh-out-loud tale, we learn along with Leader that treating employees and customers like royalty is the first step in creating a relationship-driven, service-focused, customer-centered culture . . . the very foundation for building the kind of company where employees want to work and guests come back to again and again. Why? Because they feel the kind of personal and emotional connection that just plain feels good. And that, I believe, is how value is best defined.

For today's consumers, it's all about the experience. Superior service is a key component of the experience, but it isn't the only one. Customers today expect great service, but getting it isn't a compelling enough reason for them to return again and again. So it's up to each of us to do more and be more than just another company whose employees smile and say, "Hello; how may I help you?" Rather, we need to create compelling reasons why our guests say to themselves, and others, "Why go anywhere else?"

When it comes to employees, an engaged and customer-engaging workforce will produce more profits for our companies than anything we sell. And yet, the majority of today's workforce is out looking for other jobs. Why? Because they don't feel respected at work. Their efforts aren't recognized, let alone praised, and their results are seldom, if ever, rewarded.

In this book, we get to know a company that truly gets it. *Monkey Business* is fast, easy reading. It will give you energy, it will make you laugh, and it will make you think very hard about whether or not your company truly gets it. As for Saturn, I'm happy to say that we do indeed get it. We were founded in 1985 with a singular purpose: people. We understood then, and we do now, that our guests define value, not in how much they pay, but in how good they feel, the experiences they have, and what happens to them after they walk through our doors.

At Saturn, we know how to build incredible cars. More important, we know the color of every guest's eyes, just like Leader.

Jill Lajdziak

General Manager, Saturn Corporation
Like always. Like never before.

Saturn Corporation does not endorse or assume any responsibility for this publication, the opinions of the authors, or the factual accuracy of any statements contained herein.

Acknowledgments

Our sincere thanks and appreciation to the following people:

Our readers, to whom we are forever indebted for choosing our book

Our manuscript reviewers, whose great testimonials, constructive feedback, and ongoing support made our journey so rewarding

Special thanks to the following professionals for their invaluable guidance and support during the writing process:

Rebecca Ryan, president of Next Generation Consulting and author of *Live First, Work Second*

Dr. Leonard Berry, author of the business best seller *Discovering the Soul of Service*

Adrian Gostick and **Chester Elton,** best-selling authors of *The 24-Carrot Manager*

Dr. Leland Nicholls, Wisconsin Institute for Service Excellence International

Dr. Edward Harris, Service Management Program Director, University of Wisconsin-Stout

The staff of Gibbs Smith, Publisher of Books that Enrich and Inspire Humankind:

Christopher Robbins and **Suzanne Taylor,** who believed in us from the start

Carrie Westover, who made the editorial process positive and painless

Jessica McKenzie, our publicist, who worked so hard on our behalf

Chris Sabatino, our illustrator, who brought Leader's story to life

Martin Yeeles, our designer, whose creativity served us well

Monkey See, Monkey Do

In a lush, green jungle on an island far away lived bountiful bands of merry monkeys who were, in fact, not merry at all.

True enough, they appeared to be very merry, with all their lively chatter and all that frantic swinging and leaping from tree to tree in search of golden, ripe bananas. On occasion, they actually found them!

To the most casual of observers, this vibrant jungle looked like it was the most productive paradise on any island in any country on Earth. This is why visitors from all over the world made their way through this fruitful jungle paradise to observe these bountiful bands of merry monkeys to see what they could learn . . . thus dutifully following the time-tested management practice:

MONKEY SEE, MONKEY DO

And so these eager-to-learn and even more eager-to-imitate visitors trudged through angles and thickets, clearing paths for their followers and showing them the way.

As this vanguard of curious visitors drew nearer to the productive paradise, they found that almost everything about it really wasn't as it seemed.

They observed, for example, that the merry monkeys weren't merry at all. Their lively chatter was merely small talk, and all that frantic swinging and leaping brought home very few bananas.

There was, however, one exception.

Chapter 2
Meet Leader, Follow Leader

In this lush, green paradise lived a very special monkey indeed. He was, in fact, a spider monkey with long, slender limbs and a fast-moving tail, which proved quite handy at work.

Some admired his remarkable, wrap-around tail. But this more accurately described his mind, since he was really quick to grasp important business concepts that simply flew right by his fellow workers.

By his very nature, this special spider monkey was agile, resilient, and well-groomed. He liked it best high in the treetops, where his keen vision served him well. There, he was able to spot the opportunities others missed and the threats that lurked in jungles everywhere.

And while hanging around in the treetops, he

found the very best bananas. Hanging upside down offered several different, interesting perspectives to consider in his quest for the best bananas.

With his long, slender limbs and his equally long, slender tail, all in branch-clinging formation, he actually resembled a harmless spider, thus cleverly outsmarting competitors' monkeys, who climbed the same trees every day and followed exactly the same paths through the jungle, in search of the golden bananas Leader had already found.

This special spider monkey lived with his wise wife and a few friends deep in the jungle. They were a colorful, talented troop, as all spider monkey bands are. Some were light, some were dark, some were golden, and some were the most glorious shades of red.

There was beauty in their diversity—yet another good reason why headhunters were in hot pursuit of these very colorful, quick-thinking, fast-moving, highly skilled little creatures. As a result, they were in great

Monkey Speak
swing from tree to tree
*the ability to quickly and
gracefully adapt to different
customers' needs, desires,
and expectations.*

Monkey Instinct
Some monkeys naturally know
which of their forefathers' footsteps are worth following in.

Monkey Wisdom
You get what you expect.

danger of becoming extinct (the spider monkeys, not the headhunters).

For most of his adult life, this very special spider monkey worked as a banana picker for the jungle's oldest, largest company, Republicana Banana. In fact, he was the best banana picker in the whole company, if not the entire jungle. And that's precisely how he got his name:

LEADER

Leader LOVED to pick bananas. Ever since he was a little monkey, his dream was to swing through the trees like the big-boy monkeys did, but faster, and pick bananas like they did, but only the best bananas.

Now that he was all grown up, with a wise wife and a hairy face (his, not hers), there was nothing Leader enjoyed more than being out in the fresh jungle air, leaping and swinging from tree to tree, always on the lookout for the very best, golden-ripe bananas in the jungle.

Deep down, Leader knew that he was a special spider monkey. He had to be, for nothing else explained the fact that he loved picking bananas so much. What Leader loved even more was sharing them with his jungle family and with his coworkers during their frequent breaks, just as his father had done before him.

Like the jungle sun, Leader would rise and shine very early every morning. And, like the sun, he flared up now and then . . . especially on Monday mornings.

On Fridays, everyone was happy. But on Monday mornings, that same happy bunch seemed altogether disgruntled. And that's when Leader took action, lighting a fire under their morose monkey butts and getting them primed for the great banana-picking week ahead. Whether or not it turned out to be such a great week wasn't the point. Leader wanted everyone to believe that it would be, thus maximizing the possibility that it would turn out just that way.

Leader's passion for picking bananas crept into every aspect of his life. His wise wife, Confidante, benefited from this passion and thoroughly enjoyed her delicious good-bye kiss when they left the family tree every weekday morning. Bringing their generous lips together for a good smack got each workday started on a high note, helping carry them through the long day ahead.

Monkey Wisdom
Learn and use the names of all troop members, especially your top performers.

Every so often, but not often enough, Leader's boss at Republicana would give him a monkey pat on the back and tell him that he was "doing a fine job" and "Someday, you might actually become a monkey boss yourself, and then you'll get to order all the other monkeys to find the very best bananas!"

Although the boss swung around every so often, he clearly didn't know Leader's name. This made the boss look a little stupid since Leader already knew that he was way ahead of all the other monkeys in productivity, not to mention with his agile mind, positive attitude, and fast-moving tail.

Nonetheless, hearing praise from his monkey boss made Leader very happy. And so he'd swing home to the family tree and tell Confidante what the big boss said. Confidante would listen carefully, look him squarely in his big, brown eyes, and tell Leader just how proud she was of him—all the while cleverly conjuring up one simple but powerful word: *duh.*

Ahhh, there it was again: the satisfying, little word that popped into her head, and sometimes out of her mouth, when short-sighted colleagues finally saw things clearly—the very things Confidante's insight had led her to long before. Which is why she'd known all

Monkey Speak
monkey pat
1: *desperately needed form of recognition for a job well done.*
2: *extinct in some parts of the business world.*

Monkey Speak
duh
a satisfying response, best said quietly to self when short-sighted others state the obvious.

along what a special monkey Leader was. The fact that his boss didn't get it was, well, pathetic.

Despite her "duh" moments, which Leader had experienced on more than one occasion, he looked forward to coming home and talking with Confidante. Even though she'd had a long day at work, too, Leader knew she would listen intently when he was ready to talk about his day—which, she understood, was not the minute he climbed into the family tree after work.

Leader was grateful that Confidante was sensitive to his male monkey needs, which included the requirement to remove his monkey suit the minute he got home before sitting down to read the daily gnuspaper. After a particularly stressful day, Leader would add a little papaya juice to his coconut milk as his reward for hanging in there and keeping his cool when others around him had lost theirs.

And so when Leader's male homecoming rituals were successfully executed, his big monkey smile signaled that he was ready to sit down with Confidante and talk. Because she had given him the space he needed to chill for awhile and ease into home, Leader was happy to share the day's events, then listen to his wife and learn from her. He knew that she had his best interest at heart and would not

Monkey Instinct
Female monkeys tend to be intuitive by nature. Pay attention when they say they have a "funny feeling."

Monkey Instinct
Most male monkeys, by nature, need to chill before swinging into conversation about their day. Give them the gift of the chill time they need.

Monkey Speak
gnuspaper
1: good news about the jungle, published daily.
2: less widely read and spread than bad news.

Monkey Instinct
Most female monkeys, by nature, need to talk things through. Meanwhile, they need you to listen without interrupting or offering unasked-for solutions to their problems. Let them talk and they'll usually figure things out on their own.

Monkey Speak

slacker monkeys

1: bottom-of-the-barrel monkeys who expect the same treatment and same rewards as your top performers. Surprise them.
2: creatures who do a good job of simply hanging around. Since this is their strongest attribute, one too often viewed by their coworkers, acknowledge it and reward it with a quick trip out of the tree.

Monkey Wisdom

Strategic thinkers are high-flyers. Good leaders practice frequent, clean landings. They do not leave messes for others to clean up.

Monkey Wisdom

It's your customers who sign your paycheck.

offer unasked-for solutions to his problems, as he sometimes did for hers.

Not only that, Leader knew that Confidante enjoyed his amusing tales of the big boss flying high in the treetops and, every so often, swooping down on the banana pickers and leaving a big mess. He loved it that she laughed in all the right places and didn't when the mess was her husband's to clean up.

And she'd agonize over his tragic tales of slacker monkeys calling their customers an "inconvenience" and sometimes even waging verbal warfare with them! Confidante found this appalling. She clearly knew that it was the company's customers who signed her husband's paycheck. That's how she thought of them, anyway, especially during a "duh" moment.

Most of all, Confidante would feel sorry for Leader, who was rarely recognized, let alone rewarded, for his outstanding banana-picking results.

During the last few conversations with Confidante, Leader had a funny feeling inside, and not a good funny feeling, either. He couldn't quite put his thumb on it (mostly because he didn't have one). Confidante didn't have one, either, but she did have intuition, the scary kind that female monkeys were blessed with, and sometimes cursed with, at birth.

Confidante had her own workplace issues to contend with, just as every monkey does. But she sensed, correctly, that this wasn't the time to go into them. Later, maybe, but not now.

Leader's workplace problems were far more serious than hers. Her usually upbeat husband was in a downward spiral. Confidante knew to sit back and listen while Leader talked things through.

Monkey Instinct
Female monkeys tend to experience a "duh" moment several times each day. By looking into their eyes, which are crossing, you can spot such a moment as it's happening.

Chapter 3

These Monkeys Just Don't Get It

Monkey Instinct
Naturally, some monkeys get it. Some don't. Those who get it should be frequently recognized and consistently rewarded. Those who don't should be helped out (of the tree).

Monkey Speak
highest law of the jungle
the customer reigns supreme in every jungle.

Monkey Wisdom
Monkeys should be treated and rewarded according to how well they perform.

Monkey Speak
jungle fever
1: *symptom of extreme stupidity accompanied by lethargy of the mind and the behind.*
2: *usually fatal.*

Confidante got it that treating customers and coworkers exceedingly well was the secret to business success. *Why in the world would anyone who's paying your bills be treated less than jungle royalty?* she wondered during Leader's tales of workplace woe. *Don't those monkeys get it?*

Well, no.

Some monkeys Leader worked with seemed to just "show up" at work, which admittedly is important. But, once there, they didn't seem to care that their number one job was to delight their customers by picking only the best bananas and then delivering them on time with a big smile and a sincere thank-you.

At work, Leader was experiencing a values clash of the highest order. *How can my monkey colleagues simply ignore the highest law of the jungle?* he wondered. *How can they expect to keep their jobs if they don't pay attention to the very monkeys who purchase the appealing product they pick every day?* he asked himself.

How can they not wrap their monkey minds, primitive as they are, around this basic concept? How can they not hoist their lazy monkey butts up and into the tallest, greenest trees with the ripest, richest bananas the jungle has to offer? Clearly, Leader concluded, they must have a touch of jungle fever. That isn't good. That isn't good at all, he mused.

Our managers must have it too, thought Leader. Or maybe we just don't have the right monkeys or managers. Or maybe it's not about monkeys or managers at all. Maybe it's the company's systems and processes that need fixing. Or maybe it's some of all of the above.

No matter what it was, Leader instinctively knew that if Republicana Banana was going to prosper and endure through the ages, everyone who worked there had to focus—keenly focus—on the customer.

But even that wasn't enough. Leader also knew that those who buy Republicana's bananas live in customer communities bound by shared values, shared lifestyles, shared expectations, and shared purchasing habits.

Since this is true, thought Leader, and since it's also true that bananas are a rather plentiful commodity in every jungle, it only follows that Republicana would want to know the service and value expectations of each customer community.

So, Leader asked himself, why don't they know this? And, he thought, since we call our fellow monkeys "coworkers" and they're responsible for delivering the value we think our customers want and expect, why don't we involve our customers in our business and call them

Monkey Wisdom

In the jungle, where so much is the same, you can be different by consistently creating a delightful customer experience.

It isn't about the ONE big thing you do for your guests. It's about the 1,000 little things that create delightful customer experiences. Sweat the small stuff.

Build loyal, lasting relationships by consistently striving to exceed each of your customer community's service and value expectations.

Involve your customers as cocreators of value. They know what they want and expect, so ask them.

Delight your customers. Thrill them. Wow them! Do one five-minute act of exceptional service every day . . .

. . . and ask your coworkers to do the same. In a company of twenty-five, that's 6,000 acts of exceptional service in a year!

something like "coproducers" or "cocreators" of the value they know they want and expect?

This new concept, this new way of thinking about customers, thrilled Leader to no end, which is why he continued to think about it.

What does value mean to our customers? Leader wondered. *Freshly picked, really clean bananas? Or bananas delivered on time, every time? Bananas uniquely and attractively displayed? Or the incredible, reliable service customers are treated to? The memorable guest experiences they have every time they visit our store? Or the warm, fuzzy feelings they get from knowing that their families are dining on the very best bananas in the entire jungle?*

Several answers came to mind, but not the right one. Since the telltale answer was not forthcoming, Leader patted his head and scratched his belly to ramp up his thought process.

After a few minutes of this rather primitive exercise, Leader's creative juices kicked in, along with the right answer: *It depends on who your customers are and which communities they're part of.*

With bananas as Republicana's and every other jungle company's most in-demand product, they all need to know the service and value expectations of their customer communities.

And, thought Leader, *once they know this, they can build loyal, lasting relationships by meeting and by*

Monkey Instinct

Head-patting and vigorous belly-scratching come naturally during the problem-solving process. It's also good practice to engage the mind.

consistently striving to exceed each of their customer communities' service and value expectations.

Isn't that the whole point? Leader thought. *Keep our customers coming back for more by treating them like the royalty they truly are? Delight them every time, perhaps by offering them ultra-clean, freshly washed bananas?*

Thrill them with our speedy service so they tell their family, friends, and neighbors—even total strangers!— how incredibly fast we deliver on our service promises? thought Leader. *Wow them with how important our words and our behaviors make them feel every moment we have the privilege of serving them?*

Given the facts at hand, Leader was left to conclude that his fellow workers just didn't get it. And, sadly, they weren't alone: Some of Republicana's managers didn't get it, either.

After all, there were no systems, no ropes, no vines in place to ensure exemplary service and on-time delivery of the jungle's best bananas to the customer communities that value service and timeliness more than "special" sales (which happened every day; thus, they weren't special at all).

Oh, there were funky monkeys in place at Republicana to wait on customers and deliver bananas, but not the right monkeys—not relationship-driven, customer-focused monkeys. Their focus was on other things, like

Monkey Wisdom
True leaders give energy.
They don't take it.

Monkey Instinct
Some monkeys get it. Some don't. Those who do, by nature, know how to make every customer moment count. Pay attention to those who do.

Monkey Speak
funky monkeys
1: *creatures who appear to be serving customers but are much happier doing something else.*
2: *in low demand but in large supply.*

Monkey Wisdom
Valuable knowledge, insight, and wisdom required for survival in the fiercely competitive jungle are acquired the hard way, not passed down from the Bored Room.

Monkey Wisdom
When you know your customers' preferences and purchasing habits, then you'll know how to meet their needs and exceed their expectations.

Monkey Wisdom
Monitor the flight pattern of your company's morale. If it's nose-diving, your customers and profits will soon follow.

Monkey Wisdom
The best places to work are also the best at:
- Attracting and retaining top talent.
- Serving customers.
- Making money.

"What's for dinner?" Or "I'm having a bad-hair day." Or regarding their monkey manager, for whom they too often were required to perform last-minute miracles, "Hellooo? Would it kill you to thank me for doing that for you?"

All this mismanaged monkey business greatly concerned Leader, who loved his job and thought everyone else should love theirs too. What's not to love, swinging through the trees all day and gathering the best bananas for loyal customers who paid his jungle bills? What's not to love about a job that allowed Leader and his wife to live in one of the finest, lushest trees in the entire jungle?

Leader always looked forward to the days when he found the exact golden bananas his very best customers wanted. He knew their preferences and their purchasing habits, which meant he knew a lot about his customers and how to meet their needs.

But to Leader, this wasn't enough. His goal was to exceed his customers' expectations, delight them, thrill them, and make every customer moment count.

Leader would have it no other way. It made him feel good inside, knowing that he was the best tree-swinging, banana-picking monkey in the entire company. It made his spirits soar to know that he was part of something meaningful, working hard every day, doing a good job, and providing for his little family.

In his early days at Republicana, Leader felt that he was exactly where he belonged. His fellow monkeys' lively chatter and all their frantic leaping and swinging from tree to tree made him feel right at home. But after awhile, Leader started thinking about these daily antics as interesting activities with few meaningful results.

By nature, Leader was more of a "results" guy, just as his father had been before him. This, combined with several years of his above-and-beyond efforts passing largely unnoticed, and his customer service heroics unrewarded, the jungle of mediocrity surrounding Leader started to eat him alive.

True enough, Republicana seemed to be surviving in spite of itself, and some of the long-time customers were hanging in there through what seemed to Leader the company's impending demise.

And then there were customers who had experienced better treatment elsewhere, finding numerous other sources to feed them what they were looking for.

Although the competition's bananas weren't quite as good as Republicana's, the

Monkey Wisdom
Interesting activities are always interesting but seldom productive.

Monkey Wisdom
Outcome-focused behaviors produce the meaningful results you want and need.

Monkey Wisdom
The jungle of mediocrity eats Service Superstars for breakfast.

Monkey Magic
Satisfied customers move to loyal customers when they can count on:
Reliable Service
You consistently meet their needs.
Personalized Service
You remember and use their names.
Rescue Service
You solve the problems your competitors couldn't or wouldn't fix.

Monkey Instinct

Service Superstars, by their very nature, demand more of themselves, need more from their company, and want more from their coworkers. All customers need to do is show up.

Monkey Wisdom

When it comes to building loyal, lasting customer relationships, management vision is clearer with reading glasses.

fact remained that defecting customers had a better buying experience elsewhere. And so, Leader watched his company's customer base dwindle and morale nosedive, right along with its profits.

The longer Leader stayed with Republicana, the more he wanted to either help change things there or be somewhere else.

At Republicana, it was all about profit and very little about people. Selling bananas was all that mattered, but not to Leader. Treating his customers like family was the name of his game—connecting with them and making their visit an emotional experience. The warm, wonderful kind that brings guests and customers back again and again.

At Republicana, Leader was a misfit. He knew it, and so did everyone else. He could have marched into work in a blaze-orange hunting outfit, and no one would have thought anything of it. They expected weirdos like Leader to be . . . well . . . weird. Fawning over customers and leaping around like that just wasn't their thing. They had bosses to suck up to and production numbers to meet. That was the name of their game.

And so, the day dawned that enough was enough, and Leader made the leap from wanting to be with his own kind to needing to

Monkey Instinct
Just as jungle birds of a feather flock together, monkeys who get it need to work with others who get it in a company that gets it. Get it?

be with other monkeys who thought about things the way he did . . . who loved their jobs as much as he loved his . . . who felt about customers the way he did . . . who took pride in a job well-done, just the way he did.

Still, Leader struggled with what to do about it all. For certain, he had a good life high in the treetops with Confidante, his best friend in the entire world. In fact, they were planning for some little monkeys to fill the branches of their family tree.

What more could I possibly want? Leader said to his own reflection in a nearby pond.

As monkeys sometimes do, Leader rubbed his belly and patted his head while waiting for the answer. That didn't work, so he did what leaders often do: He relied on his instincts. At that moment, his monkey lips curled into a perfect oval and out came the magic word from deep within:

MORE

Simple as that. Leader wanted *more*.

He wanted more from his monkey boss than a rare pat on the back and the predictable, annual, below-the-cost-of-jungle living increase. More from his job than a select few of the company's leaders preaching one

Monkey Wisdom
Most customers will not come back if they're treated rudely or with indifference.

Monkey Wisdom
We judge ourselves based on our intentions. Others judge us based on our words and our actions.

Monkey Wisdom
When your words and your actions accurately reflect your intentions, others will pass fair judgment on you.

Monkey Speak
slizards
dull-minded, sharp-tongued creatures creeping around every company's hallowed halls.

thing and doing quite another. More from himself than showing up every day, trying too hard to work up the enthusiasm he once had and the passion that used to drive him down the road to meaningful results. More that kept him engaged, valued, and appreciated.

And that's not all. Leader wanted to see more from some of his coworkers than a grimace when customers called with a problem. More than a grunt when their customers' problems required action.

More than, "Sorry about that," when their service fell short. More than, "Kelp ya?" when greeting customers placing an order.

How clueless can these monkeys be? Leader wondered. *Don't they know enough to flash a spirited smile and say,* "How may I assist you?" *What self-respecting monkeys who loved their jobs wouldn't be smiling all the time?* Leader pondered. *Oh, the fun of swinging through the trees for a living! It's just what we monkeys were born to do!*

So, why weren't the other monkeys engaged like Leader was? Why did they think it was okay to simply be okay? Why didn't more of the manager monkeys try to do anything about this sad state of affairs? Didn't their keen management vision allow them to see what the disengaged monkeys were doing to the business by not caring for each other, let alone for their customers? Moreover, why was he pondering these things when few of the other monkeys seemed to be giving them a second thought?

All these questions weighed heavily on Leader's mind. As a result, he would wake up in the middle of the night and take long walks in the deep, dark jungle.

Lost in thought on these late-night jungle jaunts, but well-aware of his surroundings, Leader made it a point to avoid the dull-minded but sharp-tongued slizards who crept around the midnight jungle, spreading rumors, destroying reputations, and creating issues for everyone else.

He also stayed away from the dreaded blaboons, who couldn't be trusted with confidential information of any sort.

Most of all, Leader couldn't risk running into the norangutans, naysayers all, so proudly sporting and so graciously sharing their negative attitudes with everyone around.

Sadly, Leader had to contend with creatures who behaved this way at work. But he didn't have to deal with them on his own time.

Oh no, not then.

Monkey Speak
blaboons
world-class purveyors of confidential information.

Monkey Speak
norangutans
naysayers who generously share their negative attitudes with the poor, misguided positive thinkers.

Life in a Nutshell

In a nutshell, Leader's home life was fine and his work life was a mess.

And so, after work one day, Leader took a different route home, just to see how it would feel. At first, the new path felt a little weird and a lot uncomfortable.

A few new trees later, Leader saw the most beautiful birds in all the colors of the rainbow. Their sweet songs lifted Leader's spirits, and he felt like reaching and leaping higher than he ever had before!

By this time, Leader was glad that he'd chosen a different path and had tried something new. The minute he arrived home, he tore off his monkey suit and slipped into something more comfortable. But instead of puttering around in their garden or practicing his chip shots, Leader skipped his usual chill time and seemed ready to talk right away.

Confidante eyed her husband warily as he settled in next to her, wearing absolutely nothing. This was most monkeys' at-home apparel, so it was Leader's otherwise strange behavior that warranted Confidante's full attention.

Something about him was, well, different. This new Leader seemed more like his former, better, happier self.

Back in the olden days, Leader was spirited, passionate, a barrel of fun, and ever-ready to take on the jungle world. His eyes literally sparkled, radiating energy and enthusiasm for the life he was living and the exciting things he was doing to make a meaningful difference in the lives of others.

And now, these same eyes were shining as Leader gently and lovingly took Confidante's paw in his. At that tender moment, he dropped the bomb. "I'm thinking about starting my own business," Leader announced.

Oh, the joy in his voice! But, oh, the surprise in Confidante's as she asked in an octave-higher voice, "You're thinking about what?"

"Calm down, Confidante," said Leader. "I haven't quit my job. But I have done something that I need to talk to you about."

Leader handed his flushed wife a palm frond to cool herself with. "I've been talking

with my boss about some things that need to change at the company," he said.

"Good for you!" Confidante said with a smile.

"Lots of things, in fact," said Leader. "Things like how our company isn't doing so well these days, and how our culture isn't about relationships anymore, and how we used to have fun and still get all our work done, and how monkey morale is really low, and how our systems and processes are so broken that it's a miracle we can serve our customers at all, and how we don't really listen to our guests or even ask them what they expect from us, and how things would be so much better if we just made a few changes . . ."

Leader interrupted himself, since he couldn't quite tell if Confidante was going to faint or if she was bursting with pride.

"Are you okay?" he asked.

"Better than okay," Confidante answered. "Keep going. I'm listening."

"I also told my boss that I've been feeling disengaged, undervalued, and altogether underappreciated," said Leader. "And I even told him that although my body is here, my heart left the company some time ago," he said, ending his discourse with a flourish.

"And?" Confidante asked, fanning herself anew.

"And," Leader answered, "he listened to me! Not only that, he told me that he needed some time to think about what I said and would get back to me in a few days."

"I take it he did?" she asked.

"He did!" Leader answered. "He must have taken me seriously because he came back with two interesting options for me to think through. The first is a position in our Customer Service Department. He thinks I'll like that better than picking bananas," Leader said with his toothy grin. It felt really good to be listened to and have his ideas and feelings taken seriously.

"The second is more challenging," Leader said. "It's a leadership position in another division. He wants to see what I can do to turn things around there," he said with no small amount of monkey pride.

"Which division?" Confidante asked.

"Finance," he answered. "Everyone thinks there's something wrong with the numbers."

"What do *you* think?" she asked.

Monkey Wisdom
Most major buying decisions are made or influenced by women.

Monkey Wisdom
Creatures make decisions in
one of two ways: out of passion
(desire) or out of fear.

"The numbers are right," Leader said. "Customers aren't happy and the company's losing money, lots of money," he said, "which is why things need to change."

"So," said Confidante, "You now have three options to choose from and one decision to make. Just be sure to make it out of passion rather than fear."

"Meaning?" asked Leader.

"Meaning that monkeys make decisions in one of two ways: out of desire—I call it *passion*—or out of fear. For instance," she continued, "you might decide to stay with Republicana because that's where you've been all these years, so it's comfortable there. It's also uncomfortable," she said, "because you believe that things need to change and you don't see them changing."

"And now, it's even more uncomfortable, but exciting, too, because you have two good options there you didn't have before, thanks to Manager Monkey's willingness to listen and give you something to reach for.

"And," continued Confidante, "you fear that if you trade the known for the unknown and start your own business, you might fail, which would definitely be uncomfortable. It would also be uncomfortable not to do that because you'd never know if you would have succeeded."

"Or," she went on, "you might decide to start your own business, because that's where your desire . . . your passion . . . lies. Which, by the way, is more powerful than fear any day," said Confidante.

"I guess it comes down to which is stronger," she said. "Your passion or your fear?"

"So, you'll help me make the decision?" asked Leader.

"You've already made it," Confidante said with that knowing smile of hers.

"It's true! It's true! I need to go where my passion lies and start my own business!" yelped Leader, vigorously shaking the branches of his plush family tree and gleefully imagining his life free from the constraints of a business that just doesn't get it.

"I'm free! I'm free!" With that, Leader leaped from branch to branch, did a few impressive upside-down maneuvers, thumped his meager chest a minimum of ten times, and returned to his place next to Confidante.

During her husband's admirable (to him) performance, this is what Confidante was thinking: *You might be free, but this family tree isn't.*

Still, Confidante acknowledged that the little monkey she'd fallen in love with years ago was back, better than ever. Leader's passion was back! Unfortunately, his paycheck might not follow suit. Still, he had been her rock whenever she needed him, and now it was her turn to do the same for him. Confidante told him she'd support him like the rock he'd always been for her.

Rock. Hmmmmm. Now there's an idea! Leader thought.

Luckily, this clever Leader had a plan. Taking the new path through the jungle had shown him that change is good, just as he'd thought all along. Yes, weird and uncomfortable at first. But once he got into the swing of things, Leader realized, the very change that seemed so daunting in the beginning turned out to be a really good way to get where he wanted to go.

Leader had yet another important thought. *Vines. Hmmmmm. There's another great idea for my company!*

At that blissful "aha!" moment, Leader's Monkey Business was born. Along the way, as you'll soon see, it would evolve into a bustling jungle empire.

Meanwhile, reality dawned and it was time for Leader to tell his boss that he was leaving. *Gulp.*

Monkey Wisdom
Most things are more than they seem to be. Rocks and vines, for example.

This part of Leader's plan seemed much better in his dreams, where leaving wasn't scary and things turned out just right.

"Yes?" said Manager Monkey, looking up from his desk piled high with banana peels.

Whoa! Nice unibrow! thought Leader, ever the one for details.

"So? What's that little smile all about?" said Manager Monkey. He didn't like too much smiling on the job, especially at the end of the month, when the numbers weren't looking so good. *So,* thought Manager Monkey, *he must have decided on the leadership position in Finance to see what he can do there.*

Leader cleared his throat, and then announced that he truly appreciated the options he'd been given . . . and . . . that he was leaving the company in order to pursue his passion in life.

Unibrow had a grand announcement of his own. "Well, you can't," he said. "You're our star performer."

In all his years at Republicana, Leader had been called many things, but never that. Star performer? He knew it, of course. And Confidante knew it. But Leader didn't think they knew it.

Monkey Wisdom
It's hard to imagine getting tired of being told how much you're valued and appreciated.

Monkey Wisdom
The battle cry of a true leader: *I can and I will.*

Monkey Wisdom
Follow your passion.
Live your values.
Love your family.
Appreciate your customers.
Prove it every day.

Monkey Wisdom
Be quick to give credit for a job well done. Make sure your slackers know why they're being helped out the door.

It felt mighty good to actually hear what he'd known about himself all along.

But not good enough to stay. It was simply too little, too late. Now that he knew that they knew what he'd known all along, Leader said what a star performer says when confronted with a challenge. "Actually, I can, and that's exactly what I'm going to do."

With that, Leader grinned, expressed his gratitude for all that he'd learned from Manager Monkey (mostly, what *not* to do), and went back to being the company's star performer for another four weeks.

Centuries later, Leader's passion, courage, integrity, keen vision, resilience, and hard work maintained their rightful place in jungle lore. More than anything, though, Leader was remembered for living up to his name. He followed his passion, lived his values, loved his family, appreciated his customers, and proved it to them every day.

And when something went wrong at the company, he did engage in finger-pointing, but only right back at himself. When things went right, Leader praised others and always, always, gave them credit for a job well done.

On the other hand, Leader dealt decisively with slackers and swiftly helped them out the door. They knew exactly why they were leaving for "opportunities" elsewhere.

"You can learn a lot from a monkey like Leader," admirers would say as they sat around the campfire, beating the jungle drums.

Monkey Magic

The ingredients service legends are made of:

Employees First

Treat your employees like family. Open the door for them, invite them in, say you're glad to see them, provide what they need, thank them often, and share your profits. They'll be back again tomorrow.

Customer Focus

Treat your customers like family. Open the door for them, invite them in, say you're glad to see them, provide what they need, thank them often, and invite them back.

Integrity

Do the right thing. It's always the right thing to do.

Passion

If you love what you do, you're living, not working.

Commitment

Do what you say you'll do. Stand behind your promises.

Courage

Take risks. Go out on a limb. That's where the fruit is.

Competence

Almost right isn't good enough. Exactly right is what your customers expect and deserve.

Chapter 5
Laws of the Jungle

Yes, this clever Leader had a plan.

I will set my Monkey Business apart from every other banana-picking business in the jungle, he committed to himself.

I will make my business special—so special that customers from all over the jungle will buy from my company because we show them respect and appreciation; we involve them in our business as coproducers of the value they know they want and expect; and we create a customer experience like no other. And we have really good bananas too!

I'll make all this happen, he said to himself, *by creating the new Laws of the Jungle!*

Leader wrote everything down on a great big coconut, which he placed by his nest in the family tree.

Every night and every morning, Leader reviewed his coconut-commemorated commitments. Seeing them there not only reaffirmed his commitment to the commitments but also made it more likely that he would actually deliver on these promises made to someone very important: self.

Leader knew that in order to differentiate his Monkey Business from the competition, he needed to find out what they were doing that he should also be doing and—even more important—what they were doing that he should never, ever do.

For instance:

★ Talking about having the best employees and the best service, but not doing nearly enough to make their company a great place to be . . . so great that top performers, real leaders, and fast followers want to work there and stay there.

★ Talking about empowering employees and listening to their ideas for process improvement, or expense reduction, or relationship building, or service recovery, or making their company a better place to be and then either nixing their ideas or simply letting them go in one ear and out the other.

★ Not delivering the service and value their customers want and expect because they have no idea what that is.

Monkey Wisdom
Send mystery shoppers to your competitors' organizations. It's the best way to find out what you are, or aren't, missing.

Monkey Wisdom
Say hello to your customers. Make them feel important. Involve your heart. Learn their names. Express your appreciation.

Monkey Wisdom
Best-in-class companies ensure that their biggest heads aren't wearing dunce caps.

☆ Not asking their customers what value means to them; thus, defining value and setting service standards from the inside out. It doesn't matter how simply or eloquently your company defines great value and superior service. These definitions and decisions belong to your customers.

A good way to get at this information, Leader thought, *is to transform myself into a mystery monkey and shop at every one of my competitors' stores.* Cleverly disguised as an upscale (but miniature) orangutan in a vibrant-orange Bette Midler wig, that's exactly what Leader did.

Right off the bat, he realized that his competitors were making a bunch of really silly mistakes. Simple mistakes like not greeting their customers at all, let alone with a smile, and not saying "thank you" every time a customer bought bananas, or not sending loyal customers a special coconut with a sincere "Thank you for your business!" etched on it.

How silly, thought Leader, *that they aren't doing something so simple, so easy to do, so important to building loyal, lasting customer relationships. How incredible,* he said to himself. *How just plain dumb!*

While on tour as a mystery monkey, Leader observed that, in general, his competitors were spending most of their time doing the wrong things well. *Hmmmm. Interesting,* he thought.

Their activities are interesting too, right along with their results, Leader noticed. *For companies that claim to be at the head of the class,* he thought, *the most casual of observers can see that the largest heads are wearing dunce caps.*

The more Leader shopped at other jungle businesses (and not just banana-picking businesses, either), the more he realized what he needed to do in order to build a best-in-jungle Monkey Business.

For starters . . .

⭐ He had to walk his talk every hour of every day.

⭐ He had to think of his customers as cocreators and coproducers of value.

⭐ He had to base his new *Laws of the Jungle* on his customers' service and value expectations; so, obviously, he'd need to know what they are. This would ensure that his guests would be treated like royalty, simply for buying a bunch of bananas.

⭐ He had to create customer experiences like no other.

⭐ He had to focus on the details his competitors were missing.

Monkey Wisdom
You won't get the golden banana by outperforming competitors in your injured industry. To see what you're made of, go up against the healthiest competitors in other industries.

Monkey Wisdom
Keep your Laws of the Jungle simple, short, and sweet.

Monkey Wisdom
If you're the top banana, skip the company's history in new-hire orientation and share your customer communities' service expectations.

Monkey Magic
Walk your talk every hour of
every day.

Know your customer communities. Learn the service expectations for every one of them.

Base your service standards on your customers' expectations.

Raise the monkey bar of service companywide.

Create customer experiences like no other.

Provide immediate, crystal-clear feedback on performance.

Focus on the details your competitors are missing.

Go for the golden banana!

☆ He had to raise the monkey bar of service in a jungle of mediocrity.

☆ He had to provide immediate, crystal clear feedback on his employees' performance.

☆ He had to consistently praise effort and reward results, thus giving energy, not taking it.

And so began *Monkey Magic,* destined to make Leader's Monkey Business more successful than all the others in the jungle.

With Confidante's help, Leader crafted the new Laws of the Jungle, which were simple, short, and sweet. Together, the pair gathered palm leaves, divided them into piles of seven, and carved the seven new *Laws of the Jungle,* one on each palm leaf.

Leader's plan was to personally present a palm leaf to all the monkeys he hired. That way, new-hires would know, on day one, what their customers' service expectations were and exactly how to meet them.

That was also when new-hires would learn that they would be held accountable for meeting these extremely high service standards . . . higher, to be sure, than any other company's, as well as simpler and easier to follow.

Confidante agreed that Leader's *Laws of the Jungle* were spot on. Moreover, they were more straightforward and much more powerful than the complicated policies and procedures Republicana monkeys had obviously and eagerly ignored.

Leader was determined to give his future employees a clear-cut set of objectives and expectations for doing their jobs. How else would they know if they were meeting, let alone exceeding, them?

He would offer exciting challenges that would keep his troops interested, motivated, and engaged. He would do his very best to provide immediate, crystal-clear feedback on his employees' performance. Leader would remember to thank them for their contributions large and small. Just as important, he would never forget that a contribution might seem small in the grand scheme of things, but not to the individual making it.

Leader believed that these employee- and customer-focused behaviors would give his new Monkey Business a distinct competitive advantage over all the other banana-picking businesses in the jungle.

And so, on the biggest palm leaf Leader was able to find, he memorialized what he considered the driving force behind the success, profitability, and sustainability of his new Monkey Business.

And so it was, Leader had created the new *Laws of the Jungle*—laws that every business monkey would one day look back upon and realize are, to this very day, the most important laws ever written for creating customer communities built on loyal, lasting relationships.

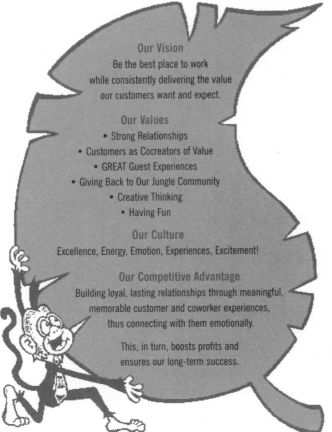

Our Vision
Be the best place to work
while consistently delivering the value
our customers want and expect.

Our Values
• Strong Relationships
• Customers as Cocreators of Value
• GREAT Guest Experiences
• Giving Back to Our Jungle Community
• Creative Thinking
• Having Fun

Our Culture
Excellence, Energy, Emotion, Experiences, Excitement!

Our Competitive Advantage
Building loyal, lasting relationships through meaningful,
memorable customer and coworker experiences,
thus connecting with them emotionally.

This, in turn, boosts profits and
ensures our long-term success.

1. Establish Your Rock

Your Rock is our company's promise to you, and yours to our customers. Everyone here is accountable for building our Monkey Business Rock and preserving its strength.

MONKEY SEE

From Our Company to You

At Monkey Business, we promise to be the best place to work by treating you with dignity and respect, connecting with you personally, meaningfully and emotionally, and having fun along the way.

From You to Our Customers

At Monkey Business, we promise to work closely with you to define value, while treating you with dignity and respect, connecting with you personally, meaningfully and emotionally, and delivering defect-free products and services on time and on budget.

YOU CAN COUNT ON US TO BE HERE FOR YOU WHENEVER YOU NEED US, FOREVER.

MONKEY DO

When you see customers who shop here frequently, learn their names. They love to hear their names, so use them often. Maintain eye contact. Our customers won't trust you if you don't look them in the eyes.

For example:
"Good Morning, Cornelius. Thank you for buying bananas today! You can count on me to be here for you whenever you need me."

2. Create Your Value Vine

Value is not what others pay. Value is how they feel. They might forget what you said or what you did here, but they'll never forget how you made them feel.

MONKEY SEE

Our employees and our customers are cocreators of the value we deliver. Thus, every link in our Value Vine is important—from our Customers to our Customer Care Department to Banana Picking to Delivery to Finance to Marketing, and everything in between.

We are all accountable for pulling together toward our Vision. Pushing causes painful breaks in our Value Vine and turns minor problems into major ones, causing long-remembered damage to others' pride and self-esteem. When there are issues to resolve, stay focused on the situation, not on those involved and what they did or didn't say or do. Do what it takes to follow the pull of our customers and then pull others along with you toward our goal of delivering the service and value our customers want and expect.

MONKEY DO

"Helen, what you tolerate, you encourage. That's why not dealing with Irritable Irvin isn't okay. Just because he isn't a morning monkey doesn't mean that he should get away with being grumpy and rude to his coworkers and customers. They all need to be treated with dignity and respect, all the time.
Can I count on you to address this with Irvin today?"

3. Live the Exclamation Factor!

Customers can find ordinary service anywhere. This is why we are committed to differentiating ourselves from all the rest by consistently surprising and delighting our guests, which makes them smile and want to come back again and again. We call this our GOLDEN CONNECTION.

MONKEY SEE

If our customers don't walk out our doors thinking or saying, "Holy Monkeys! I didn't expect that!" or "Now that's what I call an experience!" or "That's why this is my favorite place in the jungle!" we haven't made the GOLDEN CONNECTION.

MONKEY DO

"Hello, Serena! Welcome to our Monkey Business! We baked a fresh batch of banana cookies this morning. Here's one just for you and a few more to take home for your family."

4. Set Your Customer Connection Points

Connecting with customers is more important today than ever before. They can find impersonal, uncaring, rude employees anywhere, but definitely not in our Monkey Business. Here, they will find their GOLDEN CONNECTION.

MONKEY SEE

At Monkey Business, you are expected to help build loyal, lasting relationships by creating meaningful, memorable guest experiences, thus connecting with our customers emotionally. Your GOLDEN CONNECTION with our guests will keep them coming back again and again, while attracting new customers along the way. This, in turn, will help boost company profits, enhance your job security, and ensure our mutual, long-term success.

MONKEY DO

"Welcome to our troop, Goldie. We all want to help you be successful here. That's why it's important for you to know that you're expected to greet our guests within six seconds or seven and a half feet, whichever comes first. And, when you do, be sure to look for the color of their eyes. That way, you'll maintain eye contact, which is important in building trust.

"First impressions are always important, so there will be no monkey butts hanging out, ever! Be sure you tell our guests what you can do for them, rather than what you can't do, or can't find, or don't know the answer to. And, if our customers ask you where something is, escort them there; don't simply point in that direction and let them fend for themselves. That isn't what we're about here.

"We are about the GOLDEN CONNECTION—the personal, caring, considerate way we treat each other and our customers. It's all about dignity and respect, all the time."

5. MMFI (Make Me Feel Important)

Everyone wants to feel important, valued, respected, and appreciated. That includes complaining customers, crabby coworkers, and demanding bosses—all of whom want and need your understanding, your attention, and your respect. Give it to them. Make them feel important!

MONKEY SEE

When customers or coworkers seem to be vying for the "Jerk of the Jungle Award," assume that they're having a bad day and do everything you can to make it better. Don't take things personally, and remember that everyone wants to feel important.

MONKEY DO

"Hello, Maxwell. Looks like you might not be having a good day. I care about you, and I'd like to help."

6. Take Full Responsibility for Our Customers.

Own our customers' problems, requests, and complaints. When you see guests looking for our bananas, leap over to them. Welcome them, lead them to our bananas, and show them our fine selection. Our customers are your responsibility! If you can't help them at that service moment, find a troop member who can.

MONKEY SEE

Mistakes are going to happen—yours, your coworkers', and the company's. Service Recovery is critical to our success and yours as well. So, when customers have complaints, problems, or requests, do everything you can—and more—to resolve things quickly and fairly. Be sure to sincerely apologize and never, ever, say "Sorry about that," which couldn't possibly sound more insincere.

MONKEY DO

"Good afternoon, Grace. I'm very sorry that we've disappointed you. Please help me understand what happened so I can turn this around and make things right for you again."

7. Use the Energy Advantage!

Give energy! Don't take it. Set the bamboo bar high. Expect the best of yourself and others, and you'll likely get it.

MONKEY SEE

Gather ten little rocks before work every morning. Every time you give energy to a coworker or a customer, throw one of your little rocks into the jungle. If, at the end of day, all ten of your little rocks are back in the jungle instead of at work with you, you will have served others exceedingly well.

MONKEY DO

"That was really nice of you to cheer up Mr. Lizard by complimenting his green leisure suit. I'll bet that made his day."

Learn the laws.

Follow the laws.

Make more money.

Win the game!

A Monkey Business is Born

Now that Leader had created the new, non-negotiable *Laws of the Jungle* (with his wife's help, of course), he was ready. He was excited! Leader's passion for his monkey customers had never been so intense. He was itching to get to work and start building his Monkey Business.

Luckily, he had listened to Confidante's advice about telling his former Republicana customers about his new business venture. Leader believed that these loyal (to him) customers would come along and help get his new business off to a great start.

Leader was also a little sad, because Republicana was a good company that had treated him fairly well. But they just didn't seem to understand!

On opening day, all of Leader's former customers were waiting at the door for him to open his Monkey Business. At one time or another,

each of them had said to at least nine acquaintances, "Now there's a monkey who gets it!"

This is precisely why the first day of Leader's Monkey Business proved to be the busiest, happiest day of his entire life.

Not only did his loyal customers come to cheer him on, they brought their friends and neighbors! And in true Leader-like style, every single customer was treated to the jungle's highest standards of service.

For this reason alone, and there were others, Leader's Monkey Business grew by leaps and bounds. It soon became clear that Leader needed another monkey or three to help provide what his customers were looking for. So, Leader placed an ad in the jungle gnuspaper.

To his delight, Leader had dozens of monkey applicants and, surprisingly, other jungle animals too—some hoping for the chance to work for a company that actually got it and others just needing a job. Leader interviewed them all, quickly screening out the "I get it" wannabes, which included several "forget it" monkeys.

Reference checks revealed that a few of the monkeys who'd made the cut were really slizards in disguise. Some were actual snakes, who slithered around their companies

Monkey Wisdom
Treating customers like royalty breeds loyalty.

Monkey Wisdom
Unless you can tell the color of your customer's eyes during a face-to-face service moment, you're not fully engaged.

Monkey Wisdom
Your workday is filled with opportunities to enrich and inspire the lives of others.

Monkey Wisdom
Never underestimate the power of an encouraging smile, an "I care," or "I knew you could do it!"

rattling others and killing morale with their deadly poison.

In fact, one was a well-known cobra from the 'hood. He made the critical mistake of telling Leader that he'd been the first one fired from his previous job but was so good that his post-termination health care coverage was named after him!

In record time, Leader crossed the cobra, a few snakes, and the slizards off the list.

He did find the leopard candidate quite interesting, however. Sleek and attractive, she talked a good game for awhile, then moved quickly to her point. "I like to hunt, so how much vacation do I get?"

Since Leader wasn't into entitlement, this was not the kind of "I get it!" employee he was searching for. Still, Leader looked for the best in others and often found it, yet he knew that leopards seldom change their spots. They simply are what they are.

Leader thoroughly enjoyed interviewing the two elephant applicants, despite having to sit on their heads to be heard. It would have been easy to conclude that inside their big heads were big brains, but all misperceptions of this sort had been eliminated by

Leader's attendance at Republicana's management meetings.

After talking with the elephants for awhile, Leader found the big ol' boys memorable, refreshingly different, and quite capable of thinking in shades of gray.

For instance, when he asked them just exactly what they were equipped to do at a banana-picking business, where climbing trees is a core competency, the elephants responded that they would work together, power-washing the bananas picked by the spider monkeys and then hauling the heavy bunches of bananas straight to the store.

This, they assured Leader, they were very well-equipped to do.

The elephants waited, swaying patiently, while Leader mulled things over. Just then a thought resurfaced that had troubled Leader during his Republicana days. *Really clean bananas appeal to all customer communities, so why aren't Republicana's bananas really clean?*

Then a new thought came barreling through. *Maybe, just maybe, my customers will feel extra-special buying*

Monkey Wisdom
Attention goes where
energy flows.

Monkey Wisdom
Fit the job to the employee, not
the employee to the job.

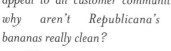

POWERWASHING
FOR
PEANUTS
EVEN WET
WE DON'T FORGET!

THIS
SPACE
FOR
RENT

really clean bananas power-washed by two enormous elephants! And so, Leader hired both of them on the spot, thus scratching his plans to hire only monkeys for his new company.

Oh, he would still call it *Monkey Business,* but Leader had learned that a monkeys-only hiring policy would be a big mistake. The two enlightened elephants had proven how important it is to place employees into jobs that fit them, rather than trying to turn employees into something they're just not meant to be.

With this in mind, Leader continued the interview process.

Next up were the hyenas who, in keeping with their nature, laughed at their own jokes throughout the interview process. A few hyenas told really offensive jokes, none of which were remotely funny and all of which were inappropriate in the workplace.

Still, they found themselves amusing, and Leader laughed at them too.

And then there was the lie-on couple—he, quite striking with his magnificent mane and reputation as King of the Jungle; she, with her fierce pride and enormous, bleached teeth. Despite these compelling features, both lie-ons had dazzling brown eyes that went for a little spin when their mouths opened wide and out poured a big, fat fib.

Monkey Speak
lie-ons
1: fierce, scary, striking creatures with big mouths and sharp, pointy teeth that mangle the truth.
2: mis-leaders.

Monkey Speak
whineoceros/whineoceri
1: animals with a voracious appetite for gossip; waste a lot of time at the water fountain, complaining about every little thing.
2: main area of expertise: blowing their own horn.
3: often miss work due to life-threatening illnesses, such as hiccups and the sniffles.
4: believe they should be promoted after three days on the job.

Dizzy from all their yarn-spinning and eyes that closely followed, Leader said something the lie-on couple had a hard time digesting: "Chew on this. You won't hear from me again." The truth stopped the lie-ons dead in their tracks.

Midway through the interview process, Leader accepted an invitation to lunch from a whineoceros, who loved tooting his own horn and pronouncing himself a "multitasker."

To Leader's dismay, it turned out to be true. The guy was simply amazing, and so were his rather widely spaced teeth!

The hungry (for attention) whineoceros managed to devour enormous quantities of food, all the while complaining nonstop about his current company, his micromanager, his lazy coworkers, his too-small cubicle and—this part took the cake—the fact that after all these years, he still wasn't the company president. *Burp!*

Leader could hardly wait to talk with the twin cheetahs, the fastest animals on the planet. *They would keep me on my toes,* thought Leader. *That's good.*

It was refreshing to imagine these well-oiled

Monkey Speak
cheatahs
1: sleek, long-legged artists specializing in controversial ventures.
2: can be spotted deep in the jungle, preying on innocent creatures.

69

cheetahs, racing around the company and swiftly executing every task on their plates. *What a challenge it would be to tell them apart!* Leader said to himself, *and an even bigger challenge to keep up with them!*

To determine just how much of a challenge, he engaged the cheetahs in thoughtful dialogue. The first twin said, "The two of us were responsible for a 75 percent increase in our former company's stock last year!"

A pleasantly surprised Leader asked, "You two did that?"

To which the other twin gleefully responded, "Why, yes. We made a killing in the market!"

Something just didn't smell right about that. These two seemed more like the slick cheatahs his father had warned him about years ago. So in one swift move, Leader sent the cagey cats, both of whom had little ones at home, back to the unemployment office.

Early the next morning he interviewed a colorful chameleon. When Leader, in listening mode, moved his head to the right, the chameleon turned her head that way too.

That's nice, thought Leader.

But when asked about her customer service philosophy, the chameleon blushed. She didn't have one, but quickly adapted and created her service philosophy on the spot. Leader's response was to stick out his tongue. Naturally, the chameleon's tongue came flying out too. Not a good way to end an interview.

Still, Leader believed the very best about everyone until they proved him wrong. And so it was with great anticipation that he interviewed a glazelle who had traveled from a land far, far away. She longed for the opportunity to do what she did best and, at last, to be appreciated for it.

Small and graceful, the glazelle glided into Leader's office and, with supreme confidence, said, "I've been waiting a long time for the chance to work for a company that gets it. I've done my homework and I know that yours does. That's why it didn't take me long to get here."

Although her words were music to Leader's ears, he couldn't help but notice that her horns were on backwards. And she couldn't help but notice that he was noticing her unusually placed horns.

"Aren't they beautiful?" she said with a smile. "My horns allow me to move just as quickly backward as forward. Because of them, I can deliver bananas to our customers

Monkey Speak
glazelles
1: small, thin, graceful beings who glide through life with a positive attitude and a keen sense of humor.
2: during childhood, trained in ballet; in adulthood, ballroom dancing.

Monkey Wisdom
Hire for attitude. Train for skill.

Monkey Wisdom
Attitude drives behavior.

with lightning speed—much faster than they'd ordinarily expect. And if I get lost, which is rare, I can quickly backtrack and make up for lost time!"

The glazelle's positive attitude and her strong commitment to speedy service were irresistible. Plus, she'd said "our" instead of "your" customers, yet another reason why Leader found just the right place for her, and for a dozen or so of her relatives, in the company's order-fulfillment process.

His final candidate of the day was the weirdest of them all. He had four legs, which was fine. But that's where fine stopped. The guy was covered with red spots and black stripes, and big blotches of yellow and blue and brown and white. Not only that, he had huge, purple eyes with gold specks in the middle. Leader had never seen anything like this before, which intrigued him to no end.

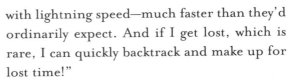

"Hello," said the colorful creature. "My name is Qwix. I'd really like to work here."

"What could you possibly do for us?" Leader asked. "You're all mixed up!"

"Exactly!" he said. "I'm a mixologist. And I'm just what you need."

What I really need is a nap, thought Leader. *Interviewing these animals is exhausting.*

"Besides," said the colorful creature, "I absolutely LOVE bananas, and I've figured out how to make the best banana treats in any jungle, anywhere," he said.

"How did you get your name?" Leader asked.

"Here, try one of my banana cookies," Qwix said. In two seconds flat, the colorful creature had slid aside the top of a big yellow blotch, reached inside and, amazingly, pulled out a soft, warm banana cookie, thus answering Leader's question.

"Very tasty," Leader said. And he meant it.

"I'll bet if you show your customers all the wonderful things they can make with your bananas, they'll really appreciate this added service. That would help set you apart from the competition by being much more than a banana-selling business, even though you'll sell more bananas this way too," said Qwix, his huge, purple eyes ablaze with passion. Leader actually thought he could see the gold specks bouncing around in the middle.

"What else do you have under those big blotches?" Leader asked.

"Oh, I have a banana pie and a few more cookies under the yellow one. And banana bread under the brown one," he said, adding "I'm cooking banana pancakes in the white one because they're topped with whipped cream.

"And there's the BARON of banana splits under the blue one! That's where I keep the cold stuff," said Qwix, who had not only thought through the bountiful benefits of bananas, he actually carried some of them with him!

"I've been thinking," said Qwix, who was obviously quite good at thinking on his feet, each of which had forest-green wings. "We could align our Monkey Business with grocery stores, since that's where all the ingredients are to make all these beautiful banana treats. Or bakeries," he continued, "or even ice cream stores!

"Here, try my banana ice cream. It's out of this world!" Qwix said, his winged feet all aflutter.

Sure enough, Qwix reached into the big, blue blotch where he kept the cold stuff and pulled out two huge scoops of the sweetest, creamiest, yellowist banana ice cream Leader ever tasted.

"Delicious!" Leader screeched, adding "Nice scoop too." Naturally, Qwix had fash-ioned his ice cream scoop from half a hollowed-out coconut shell.

"What did you do with the stuff inside the shell?" Leader asked.

"Made coconut ice cream, of course," answered Qwix. "Want some?"

Suddenly the wildest, weirdest candidate of them all became the one Leader's Monkey Business simply couldn't do without. Thankfully, it wouldn't be long before Qwix, the power-washing elephants, and the graceful glazelle and a dozen or so of her relatives would be spending their first day in the banana-picking business. Before that happened, however, Leader wanted his executive team firmly in place.

Now There's a Monkey Who Gets It!

Leader saved the candidates he knew best for last. They weren't just any old monkeys. They were spider monkeys. Some were light, some were dark, some were golden, and some were the most glorious shades of red.

Some were long and lean; some were short and chubby. Some were cuddly and cute; some were spiny and stern. Some wore glasses, and some didn't. Some sported mustaches (this bunch included a few females), and some were clean-shaven.

Leader found them all fascinating. Like him, they were quick thinkers with keen vision and fast-moving tails. They were resilient too. And their core values seemed to be in sync with his.

These special monkeys knew—they knew!—why customers should be treated like the royalty they truly are. "THEY GET IT!" Leader screeched

with delight. "Like the elephants and the glazelles, THEY GET IT!"

Two of the spider monkeys, in particular, seemed to really, truly get it. Both were strong, agile males, just like Leader, with a great sense of humor. Plus, they worked and played well with other animals.

Unlike Leader, however, one was good with numbers. The other, like Leader, was good with words and pictures.

The numbers monkey will handle my company's finances, Leader decided, *while the other will be my marketing monkey. Neither seems to be a "yes" monkey,* he thought. *I know I don't need that. And both seem to be a lot like me in some ways and different from me in other ways. That's good too,* he said to himself.

Leader was pleased with his keen business prowess—primarily, surrounding himself with good, strong executives who shared his core values and his firm belief that all things are possible, and whose strengths offset his weaknesses. On this happy note, Leader scurried home to Confidante and told her the decisions he'd just made.

Once again, Confidante came forward with a single word that said it all: *nope.*

And so Leader went back to the drawing board. Thankfully, Confidante had elaborated on "nope," explaining that he needed a

Monkey Wisdom
Placing an employee who's good with words and pictures in a numbers-focused job just doesn't add up.

Monkey Wisdom
Surround yourself with leaders who share your values and beliefs and whose strengths offset your weaknesses.

Monkey Wisdom
In a relationship-focused, service-driven culture where it's okay to have fun, employees who get it work hard and have a good time while they're at it.

Monkey Wisdom
Females lead in ways that are sometimes different from men—sometimes better, sometimes not.

good, strong female monkey on board to bring the right balance and ensure the right chemistry on his executive team.

"Females lead in ways that are sometimes different from males," Confidante had said. "You need both leadership styles to grow your banana-picking business and create an appealing, feeling culture where all the animals are working hard and having fun too."

Confidante said something else. "The female animals I know are into relationship building and leading from the heart. They're nurturing and sensitive, and they tend to be rather intuitive. Some say that females have a distinct leadership advantage in the jungle, certainly at times."

Although Confidante never, ever told Leader what to do, she made a mild exception this time: "Think about it," she said.

Within a week's time, Leader had interviewed five female spider monkeys—three of whom were good with numbers, two of whom were good with words and pictures.

In the end, he chose the female monkey most like Confidante—smart, sensitive, creative, and articulate. When

Leader asked what product she thought his business specialized in, her one-word answer landed her the job: *Relationships*.

Her big banana-eatin' grin that followed sealed the deal.

Chapter 8

The Monkeys 3 Go to Bat and Start Swinging

With his executive team in place—meaning, Finance Monkey and Marketing Monkey— Leader's business soon became the model for all the other jungle companies to follow.

They called themselves, appropriately, The Monkeys 3.

Like Leader, Finance Monkey was a strong, logic-driven, convergent-thinking male, whose favorite number was one. First in his class all the way through school, his dream was to play a significant role in the building of a best-in-jungle company.

Unlike Leader, however, Finance Monkey was adept at balancing acts. Fortunately for everyone concerned, his strong moral compass would ensure that the company's books honestly and accurately reflected its actual profits and losses.

Leader's Marketing Monkey was an equally strong, creative, divergent-thinking female with a wry sense of humor. Marketing Monkey hailed from Imagine Nation, a tiny nearby island known for its thriving toy factories and beautiful golf courses.

Playful by nature, the island's inhabitants grew up taking only one thing seriously: their elders.

Every evening the merry islanders, children included, would gather around the campfire to admire the breathtaking sunset, share the ideas that had come to them that day, inspire others with their incredible energy and enthusiasm, and end their day with a directive from their elders. It was the same marching order every time.

Nonetheless, the younger islanders would wait for their lanky, knuckle-dragging, gray-bearded elders (by now, the females had beards too) to lean forward on their haunches and close their eyes. This signaled that they were positioning themselves to end the day by whispering their age-old words of wisdom.

Everyone else around the campfire leaned forward too. They didn't want to miss the same words they'd heard from their elders every night since birth—the two little words that had made them all very special in a world driven mad by doing the same, old

Monkey Wisdom
The shorter your company's
Vision Statement, the better.

Monkey Wisdom
The shorter your company's
Mission Statement, the better.

Monkey Wisdom
Healthy corporate cultures
breed champions.

Monkey Wisdom
Dysfunctional cultures
raise chickens.

Monkey Wisdom
The best way to grow from
conflict is to stop defending
yourself and start trying to
understand your opponent's
point of view.

things in the same, old ways and expecting different results:

IMAGINE THAT!

Dutifully, the islanders would go forward and do exactly that.

And so, Leader was comforted by the values and beliefs Marketing Monkey had in common with him and with Finance Monkey, and both welcomed her differences.

The Monkeys 3 shared the same collaborative leadership style until the situation called for something more directive. And each brought a different set of skills to the table. Each was strong in areas where the others weren't, and each handled conflict (and often welcomed it) such that everyone learned from it and got to know what made the other two tick.

The Monkeys 3 debated strategic and tactical issues behind closed doors. But when those same doors opened, The Monkeys 3 were the same collegial, collaborative, effective, well-respected team they'd been before, fiercely loyal to each other.

Although Marketing Monkey and Finance Monkey thought the world of Leader, they would nevertheless hold firm to their sometimes-opposing views on the matter at hand. They weren't stubborn about it, just passionate, and they didn't take it personally when Leader disagreed with them. It did bother them a bit, however, when Leader reverted to smacking his lips and scratching his armpits, as monkeys sometimes do under pressure.

Still, Marketing Monkey and Finance Monkey gave their leader the information, along with the good news and the bad news he needed in order to be the thoughtful, planful, sensitive, well-informed, in-touch company president he wanted and needed to be.

For all of these reasons and many more, Martha's *Monkey Living* magazine showcased Leader's Monkey Business as "the fastest-growing business in the jungle."

The Monkeys 3 were on the cover, pictured in their natural habitat looking happy with their success—an image capably captured by the magazine's photographer, a snappy pink flamingo who moonlighted as a lawn ornament.

To make a point, Leader chose the spot between his two executives, thus ensuring that The Monkeys 3 were viewed by the world as the collaborative leaders they were, all in this wild, wonderful venture together.

Monkey Wisdom

Conflict is natural, unavoidable, and embraced by healthy organizations.

Monkey Wisdom

Avoid conflict today and you'll get more of it tomorrow.

Monkey Wisdom

One of your biggest challenges at work is to not take things personally.

The inside story colorfully and accurately described a business capably led by a bunch of monkeys and wildly successful in its simplicity.

Its hallmarks were . . .

- ☆ A clear Vision.
- ☆ A crisp, clean, concise Mission.
- ☆ Seven *Laws of the Jungle*, each elegant in its simplicity.
- ☆ No ugly Monkey Resources policies and procedures (especially those that require a manager's approval before someone could take action to solve a customer's problem).
- ☆ No need to remind everyone about the business hours, since everyone liked coming to work and willingly stayed until they got the job done.
- ☆ No need to harangue employees about too many sick days in such a healthy corporate culture.
- ☆ No worries about employees sleeping on the job, since the bats had been screened out early in the interview process.

And, best of all . . .

- ☆ Employees and customers feel important and know that they are valued.

And so, Leader's Monkey Business became the branch mark for all the other jungle businesses to measure themselves against. As a result, Leader and his team happily earned more business than they could handle.

Chapter 9

The First Monkey Wrench

It was time for Leader to bring aboard the employees he'd already hired. He needed to find new ones too. But not just any old employees. He absolutely, positively had to have the right monkeys in the trees and the right animals on the ground, all doing what they do best.

This is precisely when the bustling business experienced its first monkey wrench.

Leader, Finance Monkey, and Marketing Monkey knew that it would be easy to find workers who liked picking bananas and loved pocketing their paychecks. But it would be hard to find kindred spirits who shared their

vision and passion for the real Monkey Business: creating customer communities built on loyal, lasting relationships.

It would also be difficult, the team knew, to find employees who didn't cause big problems, create distractions, and kill morale by behaving like lie-ons. Or blaboons. Or leopards. Or slizards. Or hyenas. Or cheatahs. Or chameleons. Or norangutans. Or whineoceri.

Sensing his team's despair, Leader treated them to lunch at The Palms, a trendy restaurant deep in the jungle. All three ordered banana burgers, the specialty of the house, and refreshing banana smoothies served in coconut shells topped with little red umbrellas.

As the meal neared an end, Leader began with these words of wisdom: "There's the right place for the right animals in our Monkey Business." He was hoping to convince his executive team that their Monkey Business could only be best-in-jungle with more than just monkeys on its team.

Naturally, the other two monkeys agreed, thinking that Leader meant "monkeys" when he said "animals." Since this was a special lunch designed to cheer them up, both were secretly hoping that Leader would surprise them with bananas foster for dessert.

"At first, I thought that all our employees had to be spider monkeys, just like us," Leader said, "small and fast, and really good at climbing trees."

Finance Monkey and Marketing Monkey exchanged glances, wondering where this was going and still hoping for dessert.

"But then I got to know a few elephants," Leader went on. "They're big and strong, which certainly comes in handy for power-washing bananas and hauling heavy bunches of them to the store. And," he added, "those elephants have multipurpose trunks built right in!"

Leader sat back and let this information sink in. Then he folded his linen napkin and placed it on his plate, a move the other two monkeys had already learned meant: *Eating is over. Let the thinking begin!*

Marketing Monkey, conditioned to promptly respond to Leader's signals, turned her thoughts from bananas foster to another fruitful concept. *Hmmmm . . . power-washed bananas. That's cool.*

A visual being with keen insight into the nature of jungle animals, Marketing Monkey could easily picture a herd of playful elephants having a good old time, spraying big bunches of bananas and happily washing each other down in the process.

In fact, she thought, *I can develop a down-right powerful marketing campaign around such a refreshing concept!*

Seeing Marketing Monkey lost in thought usually meant that she was on the right path, Leader knew. So he left her alone and turned his attention to Finance Monkey, who was counting on his fingers.

One big elephant can carry a whole bunch more bananas than a little spider monkey can, Finance Monkey thought, quickly adding up the savings from hiring one elephant over a dozen monkeys to get the same job done.

Leader could almost hear Finance Monkey's mind clicking. *Or is that the old crocodile's false teeth?* Leader wondered. Amused, he observed the cantankerous old coot at the next table trying in vain to devour the waiter, who knew he didn't dare get too close.

Finance Monkey's flying fingers always fascinated Leader, even when they flew in public. Good as he was at adding things up, Finance Monkey had a habit that annoyed absolutely everyone: He couldn't stop himself from saying, "Here's the bottom line."

Monkey Wisdom

Trust is a fortress that takes years to build and seconds to destroy.

Monkey Wisdom

Helping others connect the dots leads them to the big picture.

Monkey Wisdom

Being helpful often means encouraging others to solve their own problems, arrive at their own conclusions, and find their own solutions.

Monkey Wisdom

It's healthier for others to digest the plan if they aren't force-fed.

No one else could stop him, either.

With Marketing Monkey lost in thought and Finance Monkey playing the air piano, Leader broke the silence by asking the pianist what he was thinking. Predictably, Finance Monkey opened with, "Here's the bottom line."

"I knew you were going to say that," chimed Marketing Monkey, punctuating the air with a devilish grin . . . the perfect setup for Leader's next comment.

"I also got to know a glazelle," he said. "She's small and fast," Leader said, smirking, "but her horns are on backwards."

Leader waited for his team's response. They knew he was making a point (two of them, in fact), so they thought before they spoke.

"Do they move around?" asked Marketing Monkey.

"Does *who* move around?" Leader asked.

"Glazelles!" answered Finance Monkey, secure in his knowledge that these graceful creatures are native to lands much farther away.

"I meant the horns," said Marketing Monkey. "Did she put them on backwards, or do they come that way?"

Finance Monkey stared at her in disbelief, while Leader couldn't help but laugh.

"They come that way," answered a delighted Leader. "But it *is* an intriguing question, just as I've come to expect from you."

Marketing Monkey appreciated Leader's affirmation, although she wasn't sure that he understood where she was going with her question.

"Well, in *that* case," Finance Monkey said, "backwards horns could be a good thing."

"How so?" asked Leader, gently probing.

"Here's the bottom line," said Finance Monkey. "Since the glazelle is small and fast and graceful, and since her backwards horns aren't cramping her style, maybe they're somehow helping."

"Hence, my question about her horns moving around," said Marketing Monkey, thinking: *duh.*

She could see that Leader and Finance Monkey were having a hard time connecting the dots, so Marketing Monkey continued. "I was thinking that if the glazelle's horns could change direction and help her move forward and backward and sideways too, she'd be just perfect for our Delivery Department."

Confident that he'd managed to bring his team along with him on the mission to

Monkey Wisdom
Fix the systems and the processes, not the animals.

Monkey Wisdom
Who cares what they look like or where they come from? All that matters is, do they get it?

Monkey Wisdom
Trust your instincts.

Monkey Wisdom

It's not about making sales, and it's not about telling stories. It's about rekindling your passion and sharing it with others.

Monkey Wisdom

A rising tide of optimism lifts all ships.

scratch their monkeys-only hiring philosophy, Leader simply said, "Aha."

Quite pleased with their lunch meeting and justifiably proud of himself for finding the best, and sometimes the worst, in each animal he'd interviewed, Leader forged yet another new path home that night.

Along the way, he stopped to smell the flowers and think about all the beautiful animals he'd hired and those that would someday join them.

Some were big, and some were small. Some were fast, and some were slow. Some were spotted, and some were striped. Some were colorful, and some were shades of gray.

And yet, thought Leader, *all the animals in my Monkey Business speak the same language! They all seem to really, truly get it!*

Nonetheless, Leader's instincts told him that something was missing. Something just didn't feel right.

Appropriately, Leader trusted his instincts and spent some quality time alone, high in the treetops. One thought led to another, a journey that ultimately took Leader to the end of the rainbow, where he discovered the missing link . . . the bond that unites all animals in their pursuit of a meaningful life.

Still, Leader wasn't quite sure what to do about it. So he scurried home to Confidante, who came to the rescue yet again. Luckily her late-afternoon meeting with the strategic planning team had ended on time, primarily because they'd stuck to the agenda.

And so, Confidante was relaxing at home when Leader came leaping through the branches of the family tree. In record time, Leader's monkey suit was on the floor and the couple's favorite coconut milk concoction was in the blender, whirring away. Leader watched as the ingredients, once separate, came together, mixed well, and emerged as one—smooth in consistency and healthy too.

"Something's missing," Leader said as he handed a creamy concoction to Confidante.

"Did you forget the papaya juice?" she asked. Confidante's raised eyebrows and wry grin signaled that she knew perfectly well what he'd meant.

Still, he said it again. "Something's missing."

"I think I know what it is," Confidante said. Her grin had vanished. In its place was

Monkey Wisdom
Swing around often and ask your troops what they're thinking. Trust that they are.

Monkey Wisdom
Listen to their concerns.

a mouthful of magic. "Remember how you'd come home at night and tell me all the interesting stories about your day—all the challenges and triumphs, all your great customer experiences?" Confidante said.

"I remember," Leader said, "but what's your point?"

Although she hated having to explain the obvious, Confidante thought "duh" but said, "Well, you didn't realize it at the time, but I felt your passion when you told those stories. I couldn't help but get excited about all the things you were doing. You were so full of joy!"

Leader's light clicked on.

"Yes!" he said. "Stories!" he screeched, turning a few summersaults. "I love telling stories! And everyone loves hearing them!"

But then, reality intervened and Leader said, "Unfortunately, I don't have much time for storytelling. But I do spend time on company strategy, so that's going well."

Leader could tell by her furrowed brow that Confidante wasn't buying what he was selling. "Okay, so I'll make time for storytelling at the end of the day, just like I do with you."

Um, no.

It simply amazed Confidante how some creatures in leadership positions could be so leaderly on the one hand and so clueless on the other; so caring at times and yet so heartless; so generous with their own merit increases and yet so frugal with the compensation of their workforce; so shameless about their executive perks and so unwilling to perkolate others; so present at meetings in warm, delightful places around the country and so absent on the job.

It was an enigma that would last through the ages—like Stonehenge, a mystery unsolved.

"Anyway," Confidante said to Leader with that special something in her voice, "It's not about telling your stories. It's about sharing your passion," she said.

"You need to share your passion with your employees every single day, instead of just at new-hire orientation," Confidante said.

"Get them all together every morning in a great big huddle. Make it a Happy Hour and spread your passion around.

"Help them catch your positive attitude!" Confidante said triumphantly.

Now she had Leader's attention.

"Make it a habit to run around the company, injecting everyone with your passion," Confidante advised.

Leader listened intently to his wise wife. He recognized an aria when he heard one.

"Swing around often and, when you do, ask them what they think about this or that.

Monkey Wisdom
Recognize their service achievements. Celebrate their victories. Reward them for going the extra mile.

Monkey Wisdom
Your small personal touches whisper to your employees how much they're valued and appreciated.

Monkey Magic

Show your troops that they're valued and appreciated. Show them often. They'll treat their customers and their coworkers that way too.

Monkey Magic

Make your workplace a joyful, vibrant, fearless, fun place to be and your business will reap the benefits forever.

Monkey Magic

In the grand scheme of life, the little things are often the most important.

Listen to their concerns," Confidante said. "Recognize their service achievements. Celebrate their victories. Reward them for going the extra mile to solve their customers' problems," she said.

"Keep your eyes open, Leader. When you see your colleagues helping a coworker or leaping to the phone on the very first ring," said Confidante, "pat them on the back and thank them every time."

Little things. Simple things, really. Small personal touches that whispered to employees how much they were valued and appreciated.

Leader, of course, knew that these were the right things to do. After all, they were seldom done at Republicana, which was— hellooooo—why he wasn't there anymore.

Still, hearing all this from his best friend, Confidante, rather than listening to the voice in his own head, brought it home to Leader how incredibly important the little things are in the grand scheme of life.

Leader was ready to say this out loud, but Confidante wasn't quite finished.

"Give them all the tools they need to get their jobs done," she said. "Show your employees—show them often—that they're appreciated and valued, and they'll treat their customers and their coworkers that way too.

"Make it a joyful, vibrant, fearless, fun place to work and our Monkey Business will reap the benefits forever!" she said.

Confidante sat back, rested on her haunches, and smiled ever so sweetly at her husband.

Chapter 10
The Missing Link

Leader was fired up. "That's it!" he said to Confidante. "That's what was missing at Republicana Banana! They had it backwards!

"Those monkeys thought their job was to serve their bosses and do what they were told," Leader said.

"They didn't get it that their job was to serve their customers. And the managers didn't get it that their job was to serve the employees who serve the customers!" he said.

"Those worker monkeys had no say in the way things were done. In fact," Leader went on, "change happened to them and, when it did, they either swung with it . . . or not.

"The monkeys who couldn't adapt didn't last very long," said Leader.

(Although Leader didn't hire the chameleon he interviewed, adapting is where chameleons do quite well as artists, florists, and magicians. In each of these roles, they're able to use color, texture, and sleight of hand to their advantage, skillfully managing change and often creating it.)

"Republicana monkeys were experts at holding grudges and never, ever forgetting a single injustice done to them," he said.

(Leader, we know, hired the two elephants he interviewed. Not all elephants, however, were suited for the Monkey Business. For example, misguided elephants, enabled by their ability to remember everything, flourish as divorce attorneys, artfully avenging wrongdoings and protecting the rights—and the assets—of the underdog.)

"Those monkeys spent a whole lot of time laughing at each other and at their bosses," Leader told Confidante.

(Although this was considered inappropriate behavior at Republicana, hyenas would have had a field day working there. Instead, most chuckle-hungry hyenas went on to choose careers as late-night talk-show hosts and producers of sitcoms with annoying laugh tracks in all the wrong places.)

"Those monkeys said one thing to each other and quite another to management," Leader said. "And when given constructive feedback on this regularly demonstrated character flaw, they promised to change but never did," he added.

(Although leopards would have felt quite comfortable at Republicana, they instead chose careers as clothing designers inordinately fond of polka dots, but convinced by their zebra colleagues that fashion statements can be made by stripes too.)

"And the Republicana monkeys questioned each decision and complained about pretty much everything," Leader said to his wife.

(Although it wasn't supposed to happen that way, some companies' whineoceri became teammates of their second-guessing cousins, the whynoceri. Sadly, this bred companywide discontent and caused others to wonder how much more could have been accomplished if the time spent on all that complaining, questioning, and second-guessing could have been directed to executing their work instead.)

"Worst of all," said Leader, "they skulked around the company, spreading rumors, lies, and innuendos—none of which were good for anyone, least of all them.

(Lie-ons would have felt right at home in the hallowed halls of Republicana. In fact, the biggest lie-ons in the jungle reached the highest positions of power at Endrun, a whopper of a company in its day, but later publicly disgraced for eating its investors alive.)

"And then there were the slizards," Leader said. "That's what I called them, anyway. They were the ones who slithered around Republicana, not meaning what they say and not saying what they mean," he said.

"You couldn't turn your back on them, that's for sure," he said, "especially if a sharp object was nearby."

(With Republicana's demise, slizards soon found their place too, reaching new lows in journalism with their popular flagship tabloid, *Bamboozle*. Bored animals who were into sensational news from unreliable sources devoured *Bamboozle*. Especially tasty were the outright lies reported as the absolute truth, doctored pictures of jungle celebrities, and ridiculous headlines like "The fascinating family of two-headed giraffes goes neck in neck with the leggy squids in this week's *Amazing Race*." What a bunch of—dare we say it?—bamboozlers.)

Leader's diatribe finally came to an end, which was when Confidante said nothing.

Instead, she offered him a golden banana—the richest, ripest one she was able to find. In yet another "aha!" moment, Leader said, "Tomorrow morning, I'm going to share this golden fruit with everyone at work!"

Leader could hardly contain himself, which is why he then did a series of beautifully executed back flips. Wrapping up his performance with a grand "Ta da!" Leader waited breathlessly for Confidante's praise. Wisely, she said not one word.

"Anyway," said Leader, "I think I have things all figured out. Employees don't need a lot," he said, "but they do need a little a lot—a little of my attention and recognition, a little of my help and support, a little of my thanks and appreciation, and a little of my respect—a lot of the time," he said.

"Hooray for you!" Confidante cheered.

Okay, so her praise was a little late, but it encouraged Leader to continue.

"Like our customers, our employees deserve the very best I have to offer," Leader went on. "After all, they give me their very best every day.

Monkey Wisdom
It's all about creating loyal, lasting relationships with your employees and with your customers.

"I expect them to find the richest, ripest bananas in the jungle, and now I have found the very same thing!" Leader exclaimed.

"It's all about the relationships," he said with enormous satisfaction. "Loyal, lasting relationships with our employees and with our customers."

Mighty pleased with the results of his soul-searching, Leader couldn't resist the urge to thump his chest. And so he did, with gusto, the customary ten times.

Confidante didn't bat an eye, nor did the hundreds of other jungle animals who recognized the sound of wisdom in motion.

It certainly is powerful, learning that when you change the way you see things, the things you see change.

Monkey Magic
When you change the way you see things, the things you see change.

The End
and
The Beginning

The Tail End

The key to passionate, inspired employees and loyal, engaged customers is found in their minds and hearts. And, not surprisingly, in their tails. In the end, that's how they vote.

When employees feel disrespected and unappreciated in the workplace, they tend to either sit on their tails and do as little as possible, or they shift their undervalued tails into high gear and, with amazing agility and flexibility, make the leap to other companies promising greener grass and employee-friendlier environments. There, they hope to find the emotional experiences and connections they need to ignite their passion, inspire their performance, and feel really, really good about where they work.

Similarly, when customers feel ignored and taken for granted—or worse, when servers, clerks, salespeople and other employees are downright rude to them—they often resign themselves to poor treatment because of price or convenience (as in, the business is close to home). Or they gladly drive a few more miles, and perhaps pay a little more, to visit stores, restaurants, and other businesses where they believe someone actually cares about them. In other words, where they feel like guests and are treated with dignity and respect every time. And, when they leave, these deserving customers are sincerely thanked for their business and not given a robotic, mumbled, "Have a nice day."

In a nutshell, here are the beliefs and behaviors needed to create a company whose employees and customers think, believe, and say, "Why go anywhere else?"

Laws of the Jungle

1. Establish Your Rock
2. Create Your Value Vine
3. Live the Exclamation Factor
4. Set Your Customer Connection Points
5. MMFI (Make Me Feel Important)
6. Take Full Responsibility for Your Customers
7. Use the Energy Advantage

Monkey Wisdom

- You get what you expect.
- Learn and use the names of all troop members, especially your top performers.
- Strategic thinkers are high-flyers. Good leaders practice frequent clean landings. They do not leave messes for others to clean up.
- It's your customers who sign your paycheck.
- Monkeys should be treated and rewarded according to how well they perform.
- In the jungle, where so much is the same, you can be different by consistently creating delightful customer experiences.
- It isn't about the ONE big thing you do for your guests. It's about the 1,000 little things that create delightful customer experiences. Sweat the small stuff.
- Build loyal, lasting relationships by consistently striving to exceed each of your customer community's service and value expectations.
- Involve your customers as cocreators of value.
- Delight your customers. Thrill them. Wow them!
- Do one five-minute act of exceptional service every day and ask your coworkers to do the same. In a company of twenty-five, that's 6,000 acts of exceptional service in a year!
- True leaders give energy. They don't take it.
- Valuable knowledge, insight, and wisdom required for survival in the fiercely competitive jungle are acquired the hard way, not passed down from the Bored Room.
- When you know your customers' preferences and purchasing habits, then you'll know how to meet their needs and exceed their expectations.

- The jungle of mediocrity eats Service Superstars for breakfast.
- Interesting activities are always interesting but seldom productive.
- Outcomes-focused behaviors produce the meaningful results you want and need.
- Monitor the flight patterns of your company's morale. If it's nosediving, your customers and profits will soon follow.
- The best places to work are also the best at attracting and retaining top talent, serving customers, and making money.
- When it comes to building loyal, lasting customer relationships, management vision is clearer with reading glasses.
- Most customers will not come back if they're treated rudely or with indifference.
- We judge ourselves based on our intentions. Others judge us based on our words and our actions.
- When your words and your actions accurately reflect your intentions, others will pass fair judgment on you.
- Creatures make decisions in one of two ways: out of passion (desire) or out of fear.
- Most major buying decisions are made or influenced by women.
- Most things are more than they seem to be. Rocks and vines, for example.
- It's hard to imagine getting tired of being told how much you're valued and appreciated.
- The battle cry of a true leader: *I can and I will!*
- Follow your passion. Live your values. Love your family. Appreciate your customers. Prove it every day.
- Be quick to give credit for a job well done. Make sure your slackers know why they're being helped out the door.

- Send mystery shoppers to your competitors' organizations. It's the best way to find out what you are, or aren't, missing.
- SMILE: Say hello to your customers. Make them feel important. Involve your heart. Learn their names. Express your appreciation.
- Best-in-class companies ensure that their biggest heads aren't wearing dunce caps.
- You won't get the golden banana by outperforming competitors in your injured industry. To see what you're made of, go up against the healthiest competitors in *other* industries.
- Keep your *Laws of the Jungle* simple, short, and sweet.
- If you're the top banana, skip the company's history in new-hire orientation and share your customer communities' service expectations.
- Treating customers like royalty breeds loyalty.
- Unless you can tell the color of your customer's eyes during a face-to-face service moment, you're not fully engaged.
- Your workday is filled with opportunities to enrich and inspire the lives of others.
- Never underestimate the power of an encouraging smile, an "I care," or "I knew you could do it!"
- Fit the job to the employee, not the employee to the job.
- Hire for attitude. Train for skill. Attitude drives behavior.
- Placing an employee who's good with words and pictures in a numbers-focused job just doesn't add up.
- Surround yourself with leaders who share your values and beliefs, *and* whose strengths offset your weaknesses.
- Females lead in ways that are sometimes different from men— sometimes better, sometimes not.

- Attention goes where energy flows.
- In a relationship-focused, service-driven culture where it's okay to have fun, employees who get it work hard and have a good time while they're at it.
- Conflict is natural, unavoidable, and embraced by healthy organizations.
- Avoid conflict today and you'll get more of it tomorrow.
- The best way to grow from conflict is to stop defending yourself and start trying to understand your opponent's point of view.
- One of your biggest challenges at work is to not take things personally.
- The shorter your company's Vision Statement, the better. The shorter your company's Mission Statement, the better.
- Healthy corporate cultures breed champions. Dysfunctional cultures raise chickens.
- Trust is a fortress that takes years to build and seconds to destroy.
- Helping others connect the dots leads them to the big picture.
- Being helpful often means encouraging others to solve their own problems, arrive at their own conclusions, and find their own solutions.
- It's healthier for others to digest the plan if they aren't force-fed.
- Fix the systems and the processes, not the animals.
- Who cares what they look like or where they come from? All that matters is, do they get it?
- One who occupies a spacious office should not be better-suited for a crawl space.
- It's not about making sales, and it's not about telling stories. It's about rekindling your passion and sharing it with others.

- Trust your instincts.
- A rising tide of optimism lifts all ships.
- Swing around often and ask your troops what they're thinking. Trust that they are. Listen to their concerns. Recognize their service achievements. Celebrate their victories. Reward them for going the extra mile.
- Your small personal touches whisper to your employees how much they're valued and appreciated.
- It's all about creating loyal, lasting relationships with your employees and with your customers.

Monkey Magic

- Satisfied customers move to loyal customers when they can count on Reliable Service (you consistently meeting their needs), Personalized Service (you remembering and using their names), and Rescue Service (you solving the problems your competitors couldn't or wouldn't fix).
- The ingredients service legends are made of:

Employees First

Treat your employees like family. Open the door for them, invite them in, say you're glad to see them, provide what they need, thank them often, and share your profits. They'll be back again tomorrow.

Customer Focus

Treat your customers like family. Open the door for them, invite them in, say you're glad to see them, provide what they need, thank them often, and invite them back.

Integrity
Do the right thing. It's always the right thing to do.
Passion
If you love what you do, you're living, not working.
Commitment
Do what you say you'll do. Stand behind your promises.
Courage
Take risks. Go out on a limb. That's where the fruit is.
Competence
Almost right isn't good enough. Exactly right is what your customers expect and deserve.

- Walk your talk every hour of every day.
- Know your customer communities. Learn the service expectations for every one of them.
- Base your service standards on your customers' expectations.
- Raise the monkey bar of service companywide.
- Create customer experiences like no other.
- Provide immediate, crystal clear feedback on performance.
- Focus on the details your competitors are missing.
- Go for the golden banana!
- Show your troops that they're valued and appreciated. Show them often. They'll treat their customers and their coworkers that way too.
- Make your workplace a joyful, vibrant, fearless, fun place to be and your business will reap the benefits forever.
- In the grand scheme of life, the little things are often the most important.
- When you change the way you see things, the things you see change.

Monkey Instinct

- Some monkeys naturally know which of their forefathers' footsteps are worth following in.

- Female monkeys tend to be intuitive by nature. Pay attention when they say they have a "funny feeling."

- Most male monkeys, by nature, need to chill before swinging into conversation about their day. Give them the gift of the chill time they need.

- Most female monkeys, by nature, need to talk things through. Meanwhile, they need you to listen without interrupting or offering unasked-for solutions to their problems. Let them talk and they'll usually figure things out on their own.

- Female monkeys tend to experience a "duh" moment several times each day. By looking into their eyes, which are crossing, you can spot such a moment as it's happening.

- Naturally, some monkeys get it. Some don't. Those who get it should be frequently recognized and consistently rewarded. Those who don't should be helped out of the tree.

- Head-patting and vigorous belly-scratching come naturally during the problem-solving process. It's also good practice to engage the mind.

- Some monkeys get it. Some don't. Those who do, by nature, know how to make every customer moment count. Pay attention to those who do.

- Service Superstars, by their very nature, demand more of themselves, need more from their company, and want more from their coworkers. All customers need to do is show up.

- Just as jungle birds of a feather flock together, monkeys who get it need to work with others who get it in a company that gets it. Get it?

Monkey Speak

swing from tree to tree: The ability to quickly and gracefully adapt to different customers' needs, desires, and expectations.

monkey pat: A desperately needed form of recognition for a job well done; extinct in some parts of the business world.

duh: A satisfying response, best said quietly to self, when short-sighted others state the obvious.

gnuspaper: Good news about the jungle, published daily; less widely read and spread than bad news.

slacker monkeys: Bottom-of-the-barrel monkeys who expect the same treatment and same rewards as your top performers (surprise them). Creatures who do a good job simply hanging around. Since this is their strongest attribute, one too often viewed by coworkers, acknowledge it and reward it with a quick trip out of the tree.

highest law of the jungle: The customer reigns supreme in every jungle.

jungle fever: A symptom of extreme stupidity, accompanied by lethargy of the mind and the behind.

funky monkeys: Creatures who appear to be serving customers but are much happier doing something else; in low demand but in large supply.

slizards: Dull-minded, sharp-tongued creatures creeping around every company's hallowed halls.

blaboons: World-class purveyors of confidential information.

norangutans: Naysayers who generously share their negative attitudes with the poor, misguided positive thinkers.

lie-ons: Fierce, scary, striking creatures with big mouths and sharp, pointy teeth that mangle the truth; mis-leaders.

whineoceros, whineoceri: Animals with a voracious appetite for gossip; waste a lot of time at the water fountain complaining about every little thing. Main area of expertise: blowing their own horns. Often miss work due to life-threatening illnesses, such as hiccups and the sniffles. Believe they should be promoted after three days on the job.

cheatahs: Sleek, long-legged artists specializing in controversial ventures; can be spotted deep in the jungle, preying on innocent creatures.

glazelles: Small, thin, graceful beings who glide through life with a positive attitude and a keen sense of humor; during childhood, trained in ballet; in adulthood, in ballroom dancing.

About the Authors

Sandy Wight, M.A., B.S., is an author, speaker, and consultant. She is also the former Director of Marketing & Corporate Communications for SECURA Insurance Companies in Appleton, Wisconsin (18 years). Sandy has written *The Road Home; Return from Depression Hell; INSPIRAGING: Aging is Inevitable, Doing It Well Is Optional; MILESTONES & MEMORIES: Seasons of Change;* and *A Matter of Trust.*

Sandy will be happy to hear from you. Please contact her at sandy@sandywight.com or **www.monkeybusiness.net.**

Mick Hager is a full-time organizational consultant, inspirational speaker, author, and professional trainer with over 20 years of experience and expertise in leadership, management, and customer service. Mick's 200+ clients include Fortune 500 companies in manufacturing, retail, and service, as well as many government agencies. Mick's client list includes award-winning organizations nationally recognized for outstanding service.

As an inspirational speaker Mick's commentary is hard-hitting and right on. He moves people to action in their personal and professional lives using his extensive experience, humor and stories. Mick truly delights, refreshes, and inspires with his wit and wisdom.

Mick earned an M.B.A. in Finance and Operations from the University of Wisconsin-Oshkosh, as well he holds an M.S. and a B.S. from the University of Wisconsin-Stout.

Mick would love to hear from you. Please contact him at mick@mickhager.com or **www.mickhager.com.**

Steve Tyink and his teams' vision, leadership strategies, and service practices have been featured in more than 40 articles and book chapters. Steve served as Vice President of Saturn Operations & Leadership Development for the Bergstrom Corporation, the largest provider of automotive sales and service in Wisconsin. During that time, the team was honored as Wisconsin's #1 Service Business of the Year and recently as *Time Magazine's* U.S. Dealer of the Year. Steve has put his revolutionary customer attachment philosophies successfully into practice, winning multiple awards. In 2004, the seven Saturn retail facilities were ranked first among the 443 Saturn facilities in the U.S. In 2005 and again in 2006, these facilities were named Saturn's Dealer of the Year. Steve and his teams won 20 National Saturn Summit Awards, a first for the Saturn Corporation. In addition to the automotive business, Steve served as a senior leader in the hospitality and golf industries and was selected by President William J. Clinton to represent the hospitality industry on the Employment of People with Disabilities Committee in Washington, D.C.

Learn more at steve@stevetyink.com or **www.monkeybusiness.net.**